The Key to
PALMISTRY

By

Leona Lehman

Illustrated by

Murray Kershner

Ottenheimer Publishers, Inc.

Copyright © 1959
Key Publishing Co.

Copyright © 1963
Ottenheimer Publishers, Inc.

All rights reserved
Printed in U.S.A.

CONTENTS

INTRODUCTION 11

SIGNIFICANCE OF PALMISTRY • A TRADITIONAL STUDY • BEGINNING THE STUDY • DIFFERENCES IN HANDS • NEED FOR DETAILED STNDY • CARE IN INTERPRETATIONS

1 THE PRINCIPAL LINES 15

MAJOR AND MINOR LINES • THE SIX MAJOR LINES • THREE MOST ESSENTIAL • THE MINOR LINES • THEIR VARIANCE • IMPORTANCE WHEN NOTICEABLE

2 TYPES OF HANDS 19

SHAPE OR OVERALL APPEARANCE • CLASSIFICATION OF HANDS: THE SQUARE OR PRACTICAL HAND • THE SPATULATE OR ENERGETIC HAND • THE CONIC OR IMAGINATIVE HAND • THE POINTED OR PSYCHIC HAND • THE MIXED HAND • CHANGES IN HAND TYPES • SPECIAL INDICATIONS • VARIATIONS IN HANDS • THE PHILOSOPHIC HAND • ASPECTS AND MEANINGS

3 THE SQUARE HAND 23

PRACTICAL AND USEFUL • SQUARE APPEARANCE • CHARACTERISTICS OF INDIVIDUALS • SQUARE WITH SHORT FINGERS • SQUARE WITH LONG FINGERS • ADDITIONAL SQUARE FEATURES • THE DEMANDING TYPE

4 THE SPATULATE HAND 29

ITS APPEARANCE • THUMB FORMATION • TWO TYPES OF PALMS • ENERGY PLUS ACTION • THE FIRM SPATULATE HAND • THE FLABBY SPATULATE

HAND • ADDITIONAL SPATULATE FEATURES • BROADNESS OF PALM • THE INQUIRING MIND

5 THE CONIC HAND — 35

ITS APPEARANCE • TWO TYPES OF PALMS • THE TRUE CONIC HAND • THE FIRM CONIC HAND • THE SOFT CONIC HAND • CONIC ESCAPISTS • MORALE BUILDERS • PRACTICALITY OF CONIC DREAMERS • HIGH DEVELOPMENTS

6 THE POINTED HAND — 39

SELDOM SEEN IN PURE FORM • MYSTICS AND ORIENTALS • SYMBOLIC OF CLAIRVOYANT FACULTIES • INTUITION • INTENSITY OF THIS TYPE • DEVELOPMENT OF POINTED TYPE • LACK OF MATERIAL INTERESTS

7 THE PHILOSOPHIC HAND — 43

THE ANALYTICAL HAND • THE TRUE TYPE • ITS TRAITS • KNOWLEDGE, THE KEY TO POWER • MODIFICATIONS OF THIS TYPE • VARIANCE OF FINGERS • EMPHASIS ON ANALYSIS • A CLASS OF THEIR OWN

8 THE MIXED HAND — 49

SIGNIFICANT OF VERSATILITY • MIXED TRAITS AND EMOTIONS • PREVALENCE OF MIXED HAND • NOTING PREDOMINATING TRENDS • D'ARPENTIGNY'S OPINION • FINGER COMBINATIONS • PALM SHAPES AND THEIR STUDY • MIXED FINGERS WITH PHILOSOPHIC PALM • SELECTIVITY OF PHILOSOPHICAL HAND • ITS RELATION TO THE MIXED TYPE

9 THE FINGERS — 53

IMPORTANCE OF LENGTH • MEASURING LONG, SHORT OR MEDIUM • COMPARATIVE LENGTHS • SHORT AND

LONG CONTRASTED • SHORT WITH CONICAL TIPS • WITH SPATULATE TIPS • WITH SQUARE TIPS • WITH POINTED TIPS • LONG WITH CONICAL TIPS • WITH SPATULATE TIPS • WITH SQUARE TIPS • WITH POINTED TIPS • MEDIUM FINGERS • HOW TO CLASSIFY FINGERS • EXTREME TYPES: VERY LONG • VERY SHORT • CROOKED OR TWISTED • FINGERS THAT BEND BACK • CUSHIONED TIPS • KNOTTED FINGERS • SMOOTH FINGERS • FINGER NAILS: LONG OVAL • SHORT OVAL • LARGE SQUARED • SHORT SQUARED • WEDGED • RIDGED • FLUTED • CHEWED

10 THE THUMB — 61

KEY TO THE HAND • THE PHALANGES • MEASUREMENT OF THE THUMB • THE THUMB ANGLE • ITS IMPORTANCE AND INTERPRETATIONS • LENGTH OF THUMBS • THE IDEAL THUMB • VARIATIONS OF THUMBS • THUMB TIPS • COMBINATIONS OF THUMB AND FINGERS • SOME EXAMPLES

11 THE MOUNTS — 67

THE EIGHT MOUNTS LISTED AND DEFINED • PLACEMENT OF THE MOUNTS • THE APPEARANCE OF THE MOUNTS • WELL-DEVELOPED MOUNTS • VARIATIONS OF MOUNTS • INTERPRETATION OF THE MOUNTS • CONSIDERED WITH FINGERS • PROCESS OF STUDY • FIRMNESS OF MOUNTS AN IMPORTANT QUALITY

12 THE MOUNT OF JUPITER — 71

SIGNIFICATION OF THE MOUNT OF JUPITER • ITS VARIOUS DEVELOPMENTS • CONSIDERED WITH POINTED FINGERS • WITH CONICAL FINGERS • WITH SQUARE FINGERS • WITH SPATULATE FINGERS

13 THE MOUNT OF SATURN — 73

SIGNIFICATION OF THE MOUNT OF SATURN • ITS VARIOUS DEVELOPMENTS • THE DEGREES OF SERIOUSNESS OF SATURNIANS • PERTINENCE TO MUSICIANS • COMBINED WITH CONICAL FINGERS

14 THE MOUNT OF APOLLO   75

SIGNIFICATION AND GENERAL DEVELOPMENT • EXCESSIVE DEVELOPMENT • COMBINATION WITH SATURN • COMBINATION WITH MERCURY • CONSIDERATION WITH POINTED FINGERS • WITH SQUARE FINGERS • LACK OF THE MOUNT OF APOLLO

15 THE MOUNT OF MERCURY   77

SIGNIFICATION OF THE MOUNT OF MERCURY • QUALITIES OF DEVELOPMENT • COMBINATION WITH APOLLO • SIGN OF PHYSICAL STRENGTH • SPECIAL DEVELOPMENT FOR FINANCIAL SUCCESS

16 THE MOUNT OF LUNA   79

SIGNIFICATION OF THE MOUNT OF LUNA • PRACTICAL APPLICATION • ITS NUMEROUS DEVELOPMENTS • UNCONVENTIONALITY • MUSICAL ABILITY • IMAGINATIVE QUALITIES • LOVE OF TRAVEL • PERTINENCE TO PROFESSIONAL PEOPLE • ABSENCE OF THE MOUNT OF LUNA

17 THE MOUNT OF VENUS   81

SIGNIFICATION OF THE MOUNT OF VENUS • ITS VARIOUS DEVELOPMENTS • THE FLAT AREA • THE SACRIFICIAL TYPE • THE INTENSIVE VENUSIAN

18 THE MOUNTS OF MARS   83

SIGNIFICATION OF THE MOUNT OF UPPER MARS • THE FORCEFUL QUALITIES OF THE MOUNT • THE NEGATIVE QUALITIES OF THE UNDEVELOPED MOUNT OF UPPER MARS • FILIAL AND PARENTAL ENDURANCE • SIGNIFICATION OF THE MOUNT OF LOWER MARS • PHYSICAL ASPECTS • COMBINATION WITH SPATULATE FINGERS • WITH SQUARE FINGERS • WITH CONICAL FINGERS • WITH POINTED FINGERS • OVERDEVELOPMENT • UNDERDEVELOPMENT • THE PLAIN OF MARS

19 SPECIAL MARKINGS ON THE PALM — 87

PLACEMENT • THE CIRCLE • ON MOUNT OF APOLLO • ON MOUNT OF LUNA • ON THE HEAD LINE • THE GRILL • SIGNIFICANCE ON MOUNT OF JUPITER • ON SATURN • ON APOLLO • ON MERCURY • ON LUNA • STARS • OMENS ON JUPITER AND APOLLO • ON MERCURY • ON VENUS • ON LUNA • CROSSES • THEIR SIGNIFICATION ON MOUNTS • CROSS WITH SQUARE • BAR LINES • SIGNIFICATION ON VARIOUS LINES • SQUARES AND THEIR VARIETIES • TRIANGLES ARE THE LUCKY MARKINGS

20 THE LINES OF THE PALM — 93

THE MAJOR LINES AND THEIR SPECIFICATION • THE THREE NECESSARY LINES AND THEIR PLACEMENT • OTHER MAJOR LINES • THEIR PLACEMENT AND GENERAL MEANING • THE MINOR LINES • THEIR PLACEMENT AND GENERAL MEANING • THE RIGHT HANDED VERSUS THE LEFT HANDED • THE RASCETTES • THEIR PLACEMENT • TRADITIONAL SIGNIFICANCE • MEASUREMENT OF TIME • ON THE LIFE LINE • HEART LINE • HEAD LINE • FATE LINES

21 THE APPEARANCE OF THE LINES — 101

VARIOUS TYPES • RED LINES • BLACK • PALE • CHANGING LINES • FORMATION OF THE LINES • DOUBLE AND BROKEN LINES • COMBINATION WITH SQUARE • WITH FORK • WITH TASSEL • WAVY LINES • MEANINGS OF BRANCHES • FRAYS • MARKINGS ON THE LINES • CHAINS • ISLANDS • SPOTS AND THEIR SIGNIFICANCE • ON THE LIFE LINE • HEART LINE • HEAD LINE • NUMEROUS SMALL LINES

22 THE HEART LINE — 107

STARTING POINTS • THE NORMAL LINE • STARTING ON FIRST FINGER • JOINED TO HEAD AND LIFE LINES • BETWEEN JUPITER AND SATURN • FORKED BEGINNING • TERMINATIONS • ON MERCURY • FORKED • TASSELED

23 THE HEAD LINE — 113

STARTING POINTS • GENERAL PLACEMENT • JOINED TO LIFE LINE • SEPARATED FROM LIFE LINE • RISING ON JUPITER • INSIDE LIFE LINE • TERMINATIONS • FORKED • TRIPLE FORK • UNDER SATURN • APOLLO • ON PERCUSSION

24 THE LIFE LINE — 119

STARTING POINTS • WITH LINE OF HEAD • SEPARATED FROM LINE OF HEAD • CHAINED BEGINNING • ON JUPITER • BRANCH TO JUPITER • INSIDE MOUNT OF VENUS • CROSSLINES AT START • TERMINATIONS • SHORT • FORKED • ENDING ON PLAIN OF MARS • ON MOUNT OF LUNA • BRANCH AT END

25 THE FATE LINES — 123

STARTING POINTS OF THE LINE OF SATURN • THE NORMAL LINE OF FATE • FROM RASCETTE • FROM LIFE LINE • FROM MOUNT OF LUNA • A FORKED BEGINNING • TERMINATIONS • ON MOUNT OF SATURN • ON HEART LINE • ON HEAD LINE • FORKED ENDING • ON MOUNT OF JUPITER • THE LINE OF APOLLO • ITS STARTING POINTS • FROM THE RASCETTE • FROM LUNA • FROM LOWER MARS • THE LINE OF MERCURY • NORMAL START • BROKEN FORM

26 PERCUSSION LINES — 131

DESCRIPTION AND PLACEMENT • FORKED TERMINATION • BRANCHES • SISTER LINES • LONG BRANCHES • LINES OF MARS • TRAVEL LINES

27 THE QUADRANGLE — 133

PLACEMENT • APPEARANCE • THE WIDE QUADRANGLE • THE NARROW QUADRANGLE • MODIFICATION BY LINES AND MARKINGS • THE UNMARKED QUADRANGLE • STARS IN YOUR QUADRANGLE

28 THE GREAT TRIANGLE 137

PLACEMENT • LINE SUBSTITUTION • THE GREAT TRIANGLE • THE LESSER TRIANGLE • POORLY FORMED LINES

29 A SAMPLE INTERPRETATION 139

INTRODUCTION

The key to palmistry consists of learning the significance or meaning of each part, line, marking, shape and gesture of the hands. This also applies to correlating and summing up to make a word picture of your findings.

Start by studying the Charts of the Palm and Fingers. Familiarize yourself with the names of the lines and look for them in your own hands. You will not find all the lines in any one hand. It will be necessary to look at other hands to find the lines which you may not have. Small lines need not be considered when first learning to study this interesting subject. As you proceed you will be amazed to see that there is a great variance in the appearance and placement of the lines.

Study the general outline and shape of your own hands. Watch them in a mirror, how you hold them at your sides, how you lift a book, a cup or any natural gesture that requires effort.

Then when you observe other people's hands you will soon see vast differences. You will note that some are large, some small, some stiff, some supple. These are the generalities that form the basis for the analysis of the palm.

Obviously, the more hands you study, the more of these differences you will observe. Each hand becomes an open book and in each case the book is a new and interesting one.

You may note similar, almost identical features between hands of two different persons. But in each individual, such features must be checked in relation to other signs.

A sharp, well-defined Line of Apollo—for example—will show brilliance; but in what direction is another matter. Two persons gifted with strong Apollo Lines may shine in vastly different fields. Further study of each hand is needed to fathom the individual's special bent.

On this account, it is unwise to jump to conclusions too quickly when studying a hand. You may note something at first sight which seems predominant, but which loses its importance as you continue.

People regard palmistry as something filled with contradictions. Quite to the contrary. The experienced student of the subject knows that one feature confirms another. The result is a fine blend that gives a remarkable reading of the individual's personality.

14   **Key to Palmistry**

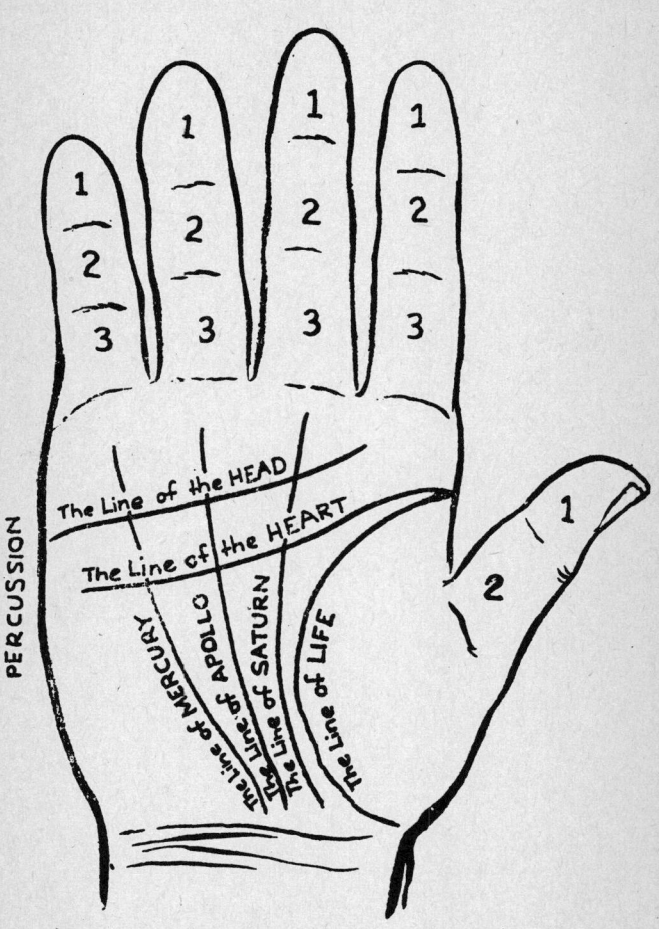

The Major Lines

1
THE PRINCIPAL LINES

The principal lines of the hand fall into two classes: The Major Lines and the Minor Lines.

THE MAJOR LINES

The Major Lines will be recognizable to the reader after studying the illustration on the opposite page. They are:

> The Life Line.
> The Heart Line.
> The Head Line.
> The Line of Saturn.
> The Line of Apollo.
> The Line of Mercury.

Usually the first three lines named above are found on every hand, though there are some exceptions.

It is rare, however, that all the last three appear on any one hand. If they do, it is a most favorable combination that denotes exceptional ability in more than one field of endeavor, marking the person as versatile indeed.

The Major Lines are the basis for interpretation of the hand, therefore they must be noted fully. Those that appear must be well-marked in order to have a strong positive significance.

THE MINOR LINES

The Minor Lines of the hand are as follows:

> The Line of Intuition.
> The Line of Mars.
> The Line of Affection.
> The Girdle of Venus.
> The Ring of Solomon.
> The Rascettes.

The chart on the next page shows all these Minor Lines and their respective names. The Major Lines are also there but not named.

The Line of Affection is also called the Line of Marriage. In many hands there will be found several of these lines parallel to each other and for this reason they are spoken of in the plural as Affection Lines.

The Rascettes are also called the Bracelet Lines. They are the lines that cross the wrist. They appear in several formations, that is, in solid lines, broken lines or curved lines.

The Principal Lines

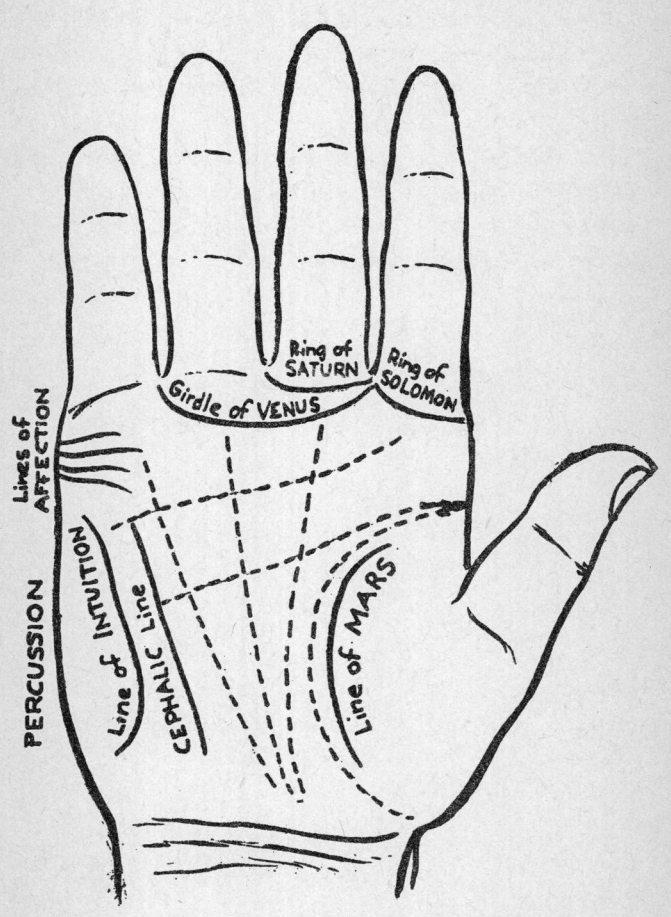

The Minor Lines

The Minor Lines of the hand vary in number and most hands show a few of them. If any one of these Minor Lines is very noticeable, then it will have importance on the reading of the Major Lines.

In the chapters that follow refer to these Illustrations until you are thoroughly familiar with all the Principal Lines, their nomenclature and their normal placement.

2
TYPES
OF
HANDS

The first thing you notice in studying hands is their shape or overall appearance. From this it is possible to study character without going into a detailed study of the palm.

Naturally, the study of hand shapes is simply a preliminary to other details, but it is highly important because it ties in with other phases of hand study and corroborates much that can be learned from the palm and its lines.

CLASSIFICATION OF HANDS

Hands are classified according to their shape. Generally speaking there are four basic types of hands as follows:

The Square Hand, often termed the Practical Hand.

The Spatulate Hand which is also known as the Energetic Hand.

The Conic Hand known as the Imaginative Hand.

The Pointed Hand, often called the Psychic Hand because of its great sensitivity.

Each of these hands in its pure form represents a distinctive type, with special traits that can be attributed to it. But, it is seldom that such types are seen in their pure or exact form. When they do appear in pure form they are often indicative of some special racial or occupational type.

The famous French authority Desbarrolles noted this many years ago in relation to the hands of artists, inventors, etc., and his findings have formed the basis of more modern study.

THE MIXED HAND

Today in our complex civilization with its many new and surprising outlets for natural talent, much broader interpretations can be given to pure types of hands. But oddly modern study also shows many composite types, which come under the general classification of a Mixed Hand.

This may be due to the fact that in the old days only the nobility represented an idle class,

Types of Hands

only the peasants tilled the fields, and workers were confined to special types of trades from generation to generation. So the early exponents of hand study actually found many pure types that were limited in such ways.

Now the trend is changing, but usually you can trace some phase of a profession or occupation in the hand of a person who has taken up such work.

SPECIAL INDICATIONS

Hands, too, are reflectors of natural indications or leanings. The result is that our modern types are changing. Just as a person's interest becomes wider or they adapt themselves to new surroundings so do their hands show it.

This age of automation will undoubtedly have a great deal to do with the changing of hands.

Increased leisure will produce a gradual softening and relaxing of the hands, so much so, that within a few generations the shape too should tend toward a modification.

The reverse has been true of many women, descendents of a long line of wealthy people unaccustomed to manual tasks, who by choice, have chosen to live in a small apartment and enjoy privacy by doing their own household chores. These very hands, still beautiful, show a broadening and a firmer skin texture due entirely to the exercising of the hands.

VARIATIONS IN HANDS

The need to examine many, many hands cannot be overstressed because it is the only method by which the beginning student can learn to differentiate the types and shapes of hands.

Another type of hand worthy of mention here is the Philosophic Hand, meaning the aesthetic, serious thinking person.

The physical aspects and significant meanings of each of the aforementioned types will be explained in the following pages.

Also there will be discussions on various kinds of Mixed Hands.

3
THE
SQUARE
HAND

The Square Hand is termed the Practical Hand or the useful hand because there are so many of them. They are existent in almost every corner of the earth.

The hand gives a general appearance of squareness. Blunt fingers, squarish fingernails, the palm squared at the base, where it is joined to the wrist.

People who possess this type of hand are conscientious, hard workers. They like order and precision. They are strict conformists to law and conventions. They have great perseverance.

These are the people who prefer practical sciences and studies. They are to be found in commerce, agriculture, and the like. In fact anything where they can apply honest, sincere effort

Key to Palmistry

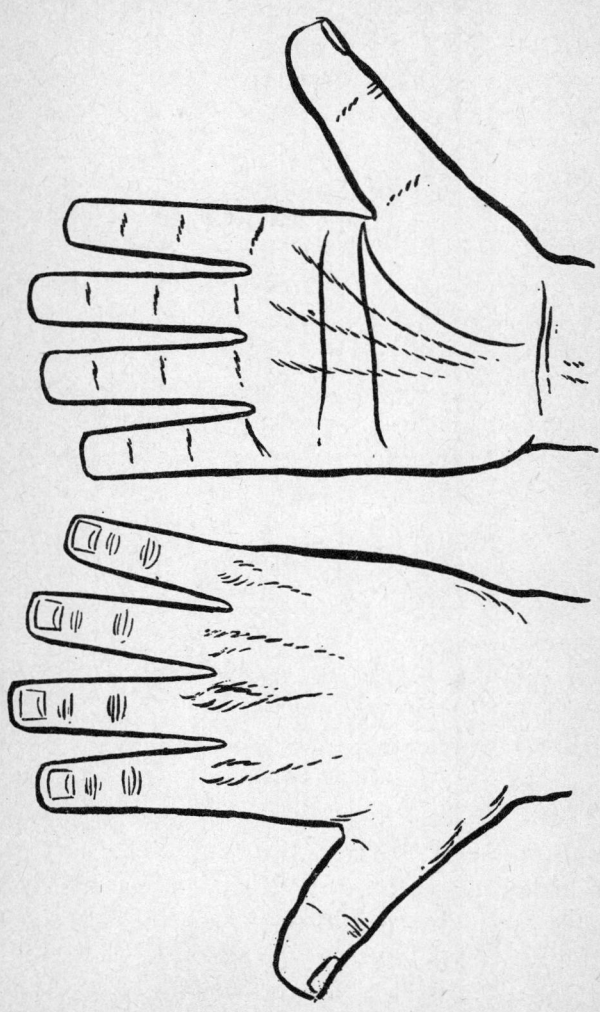

The Square Hand

The Square Hand

appeals to them and they reciprocate all of their sincerity and honesty.

Since they are methodical by nature they are easily diciplined for routine of office, school, shop or home.

Although not usually of a demonstrative nature, they are homeloving people and truly the salt of the earth.

There is a point of obstinacy in the persons who possess true Square Hands because they seem to be guided by a "yard stick" evaluation of everybody and everything. They move and act by set rules. They believe as far as they can see or know to be true or existent. Beyond that they are hard to convince.

SQUARE WITH SHORT FINGERS

The Square Hand with short fingers is very materialistic, sometimes narrow-minded. If they are connected with law they will impose their authority to the last degree. If they are homemakers, everything must be in its place.

As business men and women they are practical. They want to earn money. In fact they like to save money. Oftimes they may be considered a little too careful, even "tight" or miserly, but it is their careful look at the future that lends this air of vigilance to a practical mind.

They are definitely materialistic but even the poorest of them wants his or her little home, a nest egg and a place in their community.

These people should not be content with limited horizons. They should realize that there is a world beyond their front door. They should not disparge that which they know nothing about. Being industrious and good workers they should try to make the most of what they know.

SQUARE WITH LONG FINGERS

The Square Hand with Long Fingers possesses a more astute mental development than the Square Hand with the Short Fingers. Although the people with these long fingers have the same desire for precision and orderliness they are far more logical. They will take more time to work things out. They move cautiously, try to understand the other fellow's viewpoint even though they appear to follow the same order of rules and regulations.

They like the exact sciences and can be found as teachers of mathematics, scientific investigators or in careers where they can follow anything that involves logic or reasoning ability. If they come from a family of teachers they are likely to follow suit. They will fit to any group that teaches grammar, languages, politics or science of a type that appeals to them; in fact any place where they can exert their feeling of authority, practicality and justice.

Many of these people like to be auditors, cashiers, bank tellers, accountants, secretaries of insurance companies and such. They are useful, practical, law abiding individuals but bound and determined to follow a definite channel.

ADDITIONAL SQUARE FEATURES

Should the owner of the Square Hand with the Long Fingers have a smooth, finely textured skin, it could mean that he or she has the ability for acting or for the higher brackets in business. The higher they go the stricter they are as disciplinarians. They are excellent organizers, ethical and amenable to their superiors.

Once they have chosen their profession they will proceed methodically, systematically. Their sense of duty will make them stay with their choice of occupation. This too applies to their family and material obligations.

THE DEMANDING TYPE

As a rule, these people with long-fingered Square Hands are just as demanding upon those who serve them or who work with them. Unfortunately they do not always have such orderly and methodical assistants as they would like and it is then that they must exert every effort to maintain a logical balance.

The markings in the palm, plus variations in finger formation would indicate which particular field would be most suitable for the individual. This phase will be covered later.

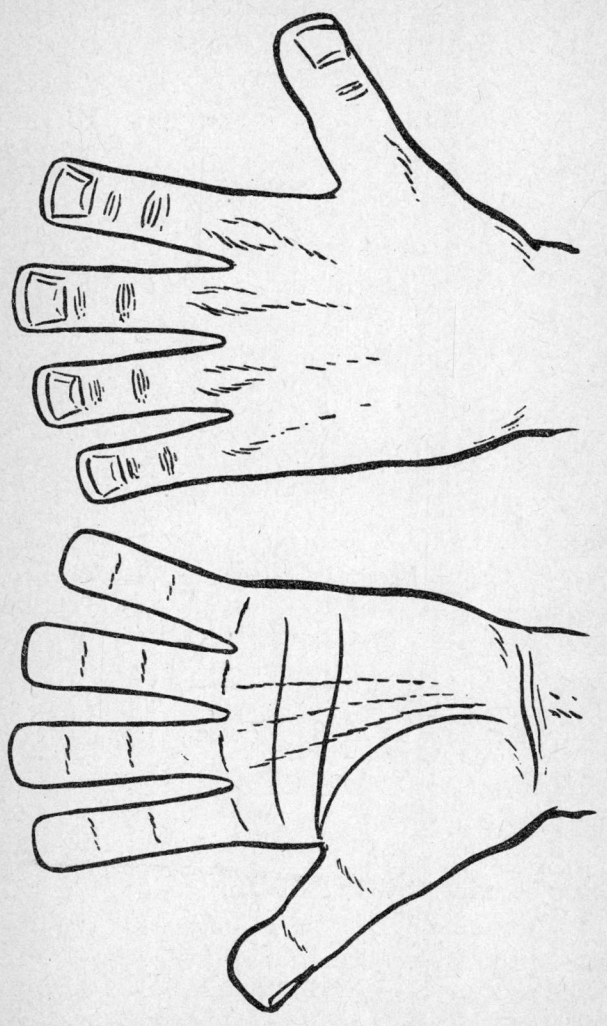

The Spatulate Hand

4
THE
SPATULATE
HAND

The Spatulate Hand is also known as the Energetic Hand, as it is representative of great physical activity. The finger tips have the appearance of a spatula, as though a slight flattening has caused them to widen out. From this, the hand has gained its descriptive title.

With this type of hand, the thumbs are noticeably large. The palm may be of two forms and still be a true Spatulate type. In one form, the palm is wider at the wrist than at the base of the fingers, but the finger tips themselves must be marked Spatulate appearance.

In the other form, the palm is wider at the base of the fingers than at the wrist, thus giving the hand a fan shape. The fingers seem to spread out, adding to the overall effect.

ENERGY PLUS ACTION

People with Spatulate Hands have an abundance of energy. They are always restless because of their love for action. They are also characterized by their desire for independence. They are capable of making so many things—either as creators or as copyists—that they feel no need for dependence upon any one.

They shun any interference in their plans or affairs, so petulant persons with such hands must be handled carefully and tactfully.

When a Spatulate Hand is firm and hard, it shows a yearning for travel that can carry into fields of exploration or some place in navigation, aviation, engineering, etc. This applies to women as well. They may be in the theatre as an actress or a singer; such a person might be a nurse or a milliner, but in each case there will be the desire to do something new, unheard of, or there may be the feeling that travel must be added to their talent.

THE FIRM SPATULATE HANDS

In each instance a wider field of activity results so the nurse might become a stewardess aboard a ship or airplane, the milliner might create her own models and tour the country making presentations in stores from coast to coast. The actress and singer could be restless indeed if denied the opportunity to travel round

The Spatulate Hand

the world. These are just a few examples of the Spatulate type hand.

These are the enthusiastic class looking for new ideas, new scenes. They are never satisfied with monotony, they want action, so for this reason alone they will find some new interest or activity. It is possible for these people to find themselves in a business position where they are really in a monotonous form of occupation, but they find time to take up a hobby that fills their desire for creativeness and thus achieve a balanced form of living.

THE FLABBY SPATULATE HAND

When the Spatulate Hand is flabby and soft, the restless nature becomes changeable, dissatisfied and really irritable. They may start many things or projects but seldom finish them. They must learn to concentrate on one thing at a time.

The longer the fingers on the Spatulate Hand the more independent and individualistic the person will be. Whatever the particular talent may be, there will be a desire to exceed anything that has been done by anyone else. This is the reason for explorers and navigators. The urge to see the unknown, to experience something that no one else has ever seen or done.

This spirit of achievement lies also in the mind of the mechanic or the carpenter or the watchmaker, etc., so each in turn may become an inventor.

ADDITIONAL SPATULATE FEATURES

When the fingers are too long the state of mind trends toward the abnormal, so there develops the overenthusiastic person who can become a crank or just plain crotchety. If however there is this finger formation combined with a strong thumb, then there will be the ability to look ahead, to forsee new ways of doing things. This is how leaders in new thought, new publicity, new inventions push into prominence. It is their intense activity and independence of thought that produces their visionary talent.

When the palm is broader at the base of the fingers there is more practicality. These are the people who like to use their hands to make things. This includes the entire group, that is from the smallest even though it be just the woman who sews at home or the man who makes things in his home workshop to the top line inventor of the automobile or best selling gadget.

If the palm of the hand is broader at the base of the hand, at the wrist, then the creative ability is often applied to ideas. The talent may be publicity, the person with ideas to sell national products or stunts to promote a movie star or a television personality.

If a person is religious then the trend would be something new or sparkling in the treatment of religion. These were the sparks that produced so many varying religious sects. New philosophies sprang into being because of independent thinkers who had this restless tenacity and power. Courageous sea captains belong to this class too. Never will they look back. Always they look into the future. No doubt many of these adventurous men and women will be devoting themselves to the exploration of the unknown world of the planets.

34   Key to Palmistry

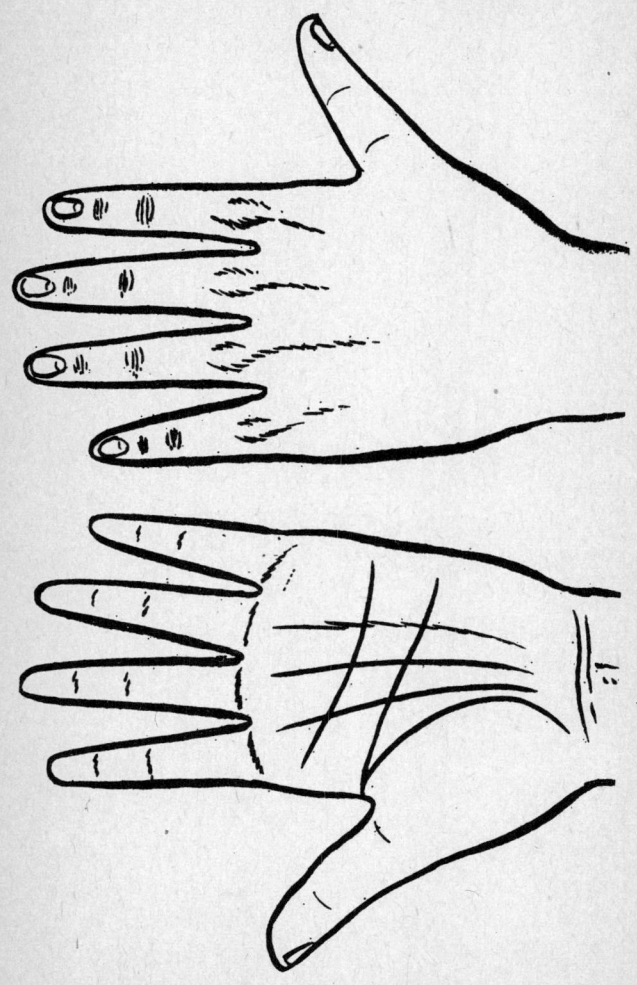

The Conic Hand

5
THE
CONIC
HAND

The Conic Hand, known as the artistic hand, indicates an emotional nature. In its purest form it is highly imaginative.

Persons with Conic Hands love everything that is beautiful. They become inspired by beauty itself and for this reason they want beautiful surroundings.

THE TRUE CONIC HAND

The true Conic Hand has smooth fingers that taper from the base of each finger, gradually lessening toward the tip. The tips are always rounded, never pointed. Also remember the fingers must be smooth, never knotty, never any bumpy joints nor heavy knuckle formation.

People of this type are fortunate to have both

intuition and a vivid imagination. They are often too impulsive because they are too enthusiastic. They do not like to spend time trying to rationalize things.

When they are in a convivial mood they make charming companions, but when they have anything that is discouraging they sink to the depths of despair. They have the ability to change their moods very rapidly. Many people of the theater and music world have hands of this type.

A housewife with this type hand does not like menial chores but she always finds a way to keep her home and surroundings artistically attractive.

THE FIRM CONIC HAND

The Conic Hand also represents the dreamer. With a firm palm these dreams are accompanied with a quick mentality. Art, music, literature, or any artistic profession appeals to persons with the Conic Hand that has firm palms.

THE SOFT CONIC HAND

When the hand is soft the palm is likely to be somewhat spongy. In this case there will be self-indulgence, impracticality and a dreaminess that may incline toward laziness. Often it is possible to observe the hands of men and women in restaurants, stores, busses, or just passing by on the street. Among them you will see pudgy, beautiful examples of this indolent type of hand. They eat rich foods, drink too much, exercise too little and so on. These are the too soft, conic type hands. This is the exceptional, the unusual group of this artistic class of people.

The strong type can also be found in business offices. They work conscientiously and usually remain many years in one position. However here again they must have pleasant surroundings and harmonious co-workers. They find a way to express their great interest in artistic things when they are away from their office routine. They are to be found in art classes, language classes, music studios, etc., whenever they can squeeze in the time for lessons.

CONIC ESCAPISTS

The auther has interviewed girls who have not neglected their office duties, yet who have found time to study outside and actually succeed in making a second career. Others just gain happiness and satisfaction by patronizing the theater or visiting museums.

Men with this same desire for the artistic likewise find a great deal of happiness outside the limits of their routine business life. Hi-fi experts have been developed in the "after-five" and "weekend" hours.

MORALE BUILDERS

These are forms of escape to some degree but

it is the kind that supplies happiness and builds up morale. Whether it be a desire to study paintings, to listen to music, or perform it, to dance or just watch dancing, all is conducive to good living.

Some possess a love of color in nature, so we find they are bird-watchers or pet fanciers. All are outlets for the expression of their love of beauty.

PRACTICALITY OF CONIC DREAMERS

Hands of this category are to be found in the medical and dental professions, also in law. Again these people find their relaxation in something that is artistic and colorful to them. The culture and study of flowers, fruits and plants are not to be omitted here. One well known physician took an interest in the culture of lilies and became so expert that he gives lectures on the subject.

Architects and poets are to be found with fine types of Conic Hands. The highly developed and the well educated of the Conic class are among the most interesting and intelligent people all over the world. One has only to study hands to learn this fact.

6
THE POINTED HAND

The Pointed Hand is classified as the Psychic Hand. It is an exaggeration of the Conic Hand. The fingers are long and slender. The finger and thumb tips are pointed. It is a truly beautiful hand that is narrow and long, with exquisite tapering fingers.

This type hand is seldom seen in its perfect and purest form. This hand is fragile and so are the people who possess them. They are very spiritual so it is natural that they should find great interest, even solace, in religion. Mystics of the East have these hands. Many of the philosophical Oriental people fall into this class. Devout members of all sects have among their numbers some excellent examples of Pointed Hands, the true psychic natures.

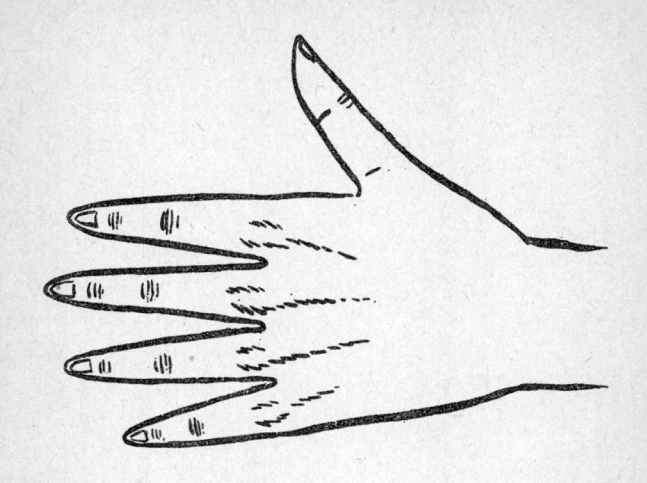

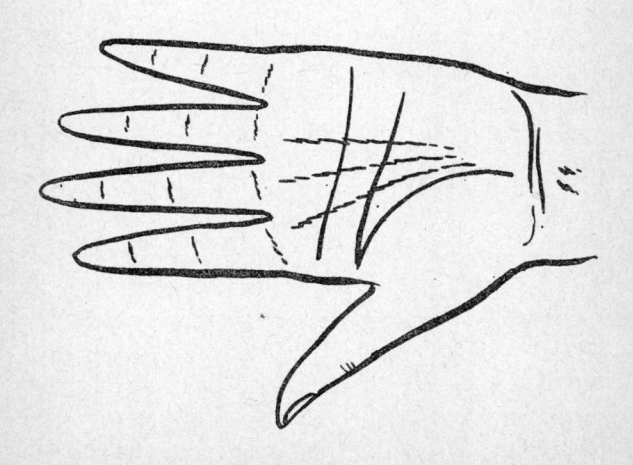

The Pointed Hand

The Pointed Hand

These are the highly sensitive souls that become morbid and melancholy if misunderstood or denied their inborn desire to worship in silence or seclusion. They love the mysterious. They also possess the ability to delve into the so-called world of the supernatural. Clairvoyants and mediums usually have a modified form of the Pointed Hand. They have tremendous intuitive powers. They are quickly impressed and such impressions seem to have an indelible quality that remains in their minds.

INTENSITY OF THIS TYPE

Just as the conic hand represents the emotional nature, so does the Pointed Hand but to a much more intensive degree. Music and color mean so much to the person with the Pointed, psychic hand. A phrase of music that is light and gay causes an immediate reaction, that of great joy. If music be sad, then in equal intensity, melancholy will pervade the mind, and persist for a long period.

Children of this type are frequently misunderstood not only by nurses and teachers but by their very own parents. Children with Pointed Hands are rare and, in America, are born of parents with practical or mixed hands. As a result the impossible is demanded of this very sensitive, intuitive child. The parents cannot understand the child and vice versa—the child cannot possibly understand the parents.

DEVELOPMENT OF POINTED TYPE

When maturity comes, such young men and women may be forced to enter the business world where they do not fit. Even if they enter a family business they simply cannot follow the so-called footsteps of the parent. Fortunately today there are psychiatrists who can help these people.

Essentially this might be called a type that seeks some kind of religious expression. It is a quiet gentle nature that loves repose and quiet. The strongest of these may be found as the head of a religious order. The least of these may be a quiet reserved person who simply helps others to find some glimpse of happiness in a world of struggle and strife.

Material things are of little interest to these people. Many of them have given their all to the church and retreated to a life of prayers and worship.

Variations of this type will be included in the discussion of Mixed Hands.

7
THE PHILOSOPHIC HAND

The Philosophic Hand is the analytical hand, always sifting facts, searching for the truth. The appearance and shape of the hand is angular. Long palm and long fingers with knotty, bumpy looking joints are the characteristic features of the hand. The fingers are firm, almost with a feeling of being completely bony. The nails are long with a squarish rather than oval tip.

The true type must have all joints developed to the degree of a knotlike appearance. It is these knots that add the desire for wisdom, plus an analytical, inquiring mind. This hand is to be found among teachers, philsophers, the clergy, in fact, in any field where an analytical mind is a necessity. Chemists too can have such hands. People with such hands like to "dig deep" and

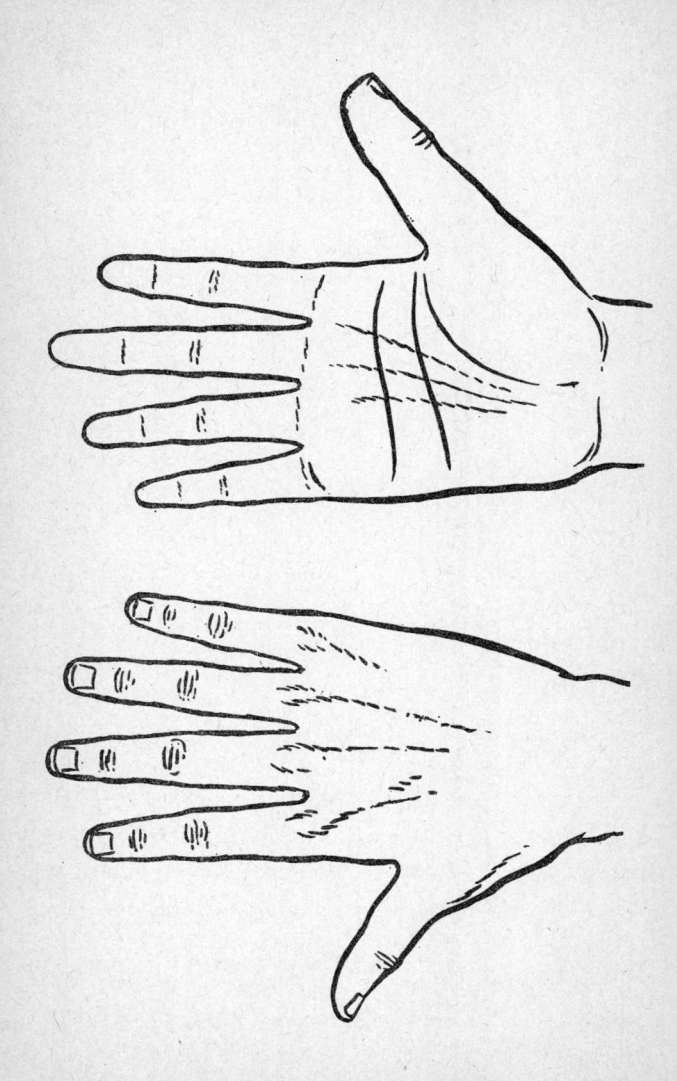

The Philosophic Hand

The Philosophic Hand

form their own conclusions. They insist upon trying, examining, prying and so on until they have satisfied themselves that a thing, project, a theory, a formula, etc., is just what it is supposed to be.

They are materialistic only to the degree of mental and physical order. They feel that "there must be a place for everything and everything in its place." This applies to mathematician, a blueprint expert or a clergyman with this type of hand. These are not the extremists of the pointed type hand, nor are they the emotional enthusiasts of the conic type. They are practical, philosophical, analytical people. They have the ability to rise above their comrades or co-workers because they have exceptional ability. They never lose the drive of the ambitious student who always seeks more and more information, more knowledge.

KNOWLEDGE IS THE KEY TO POWER

Money never seems to be their ambition, just a broadening of their knowledge in whatever profession or occupation which interests them. That often brings them money as well as success.

Their thumbs are always large and well balanced so they have the ability to be leaders wherever they are. They are methodical in thought and action.

The Philosophical Type represents a group of people who have the gift of understanding, a thing so rare. They are a wonderful balance wheel wherever they may be, and they really are in abundance.

MODIFICATIONS OF THE PHILOSOPHIC HAND

Modifications of the Philosophic Hand may be noted in the appearance of the finger tips. As already noted, these have a squarish appearance in the true Philosophic Hand.

But it should by no means be confused with the Square Hand. They have an element in common; their practicality, but where the square type is a plodder and a money-getter, the Philosophic Hand, as already stated, goes beyond such mundane matters.

Sometimes a Philosophic Hand shows finger tips that vary from the squarish. These form interesting sidelights where the personality of the individual is concerned.

If the fingers of the Philosophic Hand show a conic trend, it means a lessening of analytical ability and often a somewhat emotional nature as well.

Not that such people lack the ability to analyze. It is just that they may fail to exercise it. They lose some of the calm, collected manner that is so important to the formation of sound judgment.

Often, too, those conic tips will show a tend-

The Philosophic Hand

ency to enter more humane fields of endeavor, but still the analytical power is in the fore, even when it reaches a visionary stage.

VARIATION OF FINGERS

When the Philosophic Hand has fingers that suggest the spatulate type, we naturally expect—and find—a person who is energetic in all these processes of analysis. Such people want to see results in what they do.

The Philosophic Hand seldom—if ever—has fingers that resemble the pointed type, so there is no need to go into details on that score.

Always bear in mind that those long, bony fingers represent analysis. That is the keynote to the whole thing. It is what makes the Philosophic Hand a type unto itself, one that can be quickly recognized. Also, by a curious coincidence it is a type that can be quickly analyzed.

Variations in the tips are therefore subordinate, yet worthy of note in a hand that is representative of such a keen, inquiring nature. Little differences can lead to great decisions with persons of this category.

Philosophic Hands remain an important class of their own and however they vary, they should not be regarded as Mixed Hands, which form the next subject of discussion.

48 Key to Palmistry

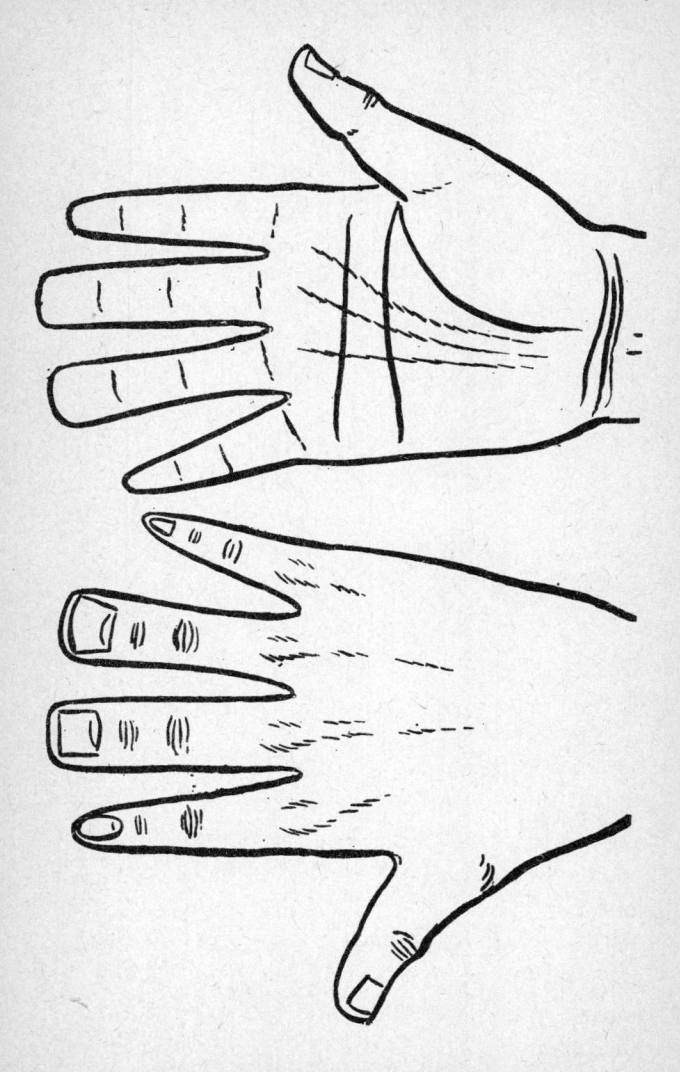

The Mixed Hand

8 THE MIXED HAND

The Mixed Hand is exactly what the title implies; mixed in many numerous combinations of the various types of hands. It signifies versatility.

Where there is such a mixing of all races there is naturally a mixing of physical and mental characteristics. The chances of finding pure hand types are indeed slim, however it is more interesting to see and study the many combinations.

The key to analyzing is first to classify the shape of the hand generally, then be sure of the fingers. You may find these conic, one pointed, plus a square tipped thumb, or just for the sake of visualization it may be two square, one spatulate, one conic, plus a conic thumb. You add up the general qualities of each of these types and get a general idea as to the tendencies of the combination. It is somewhat like adding up a number of pictures. Each one tells a story of its own.

There are times when it is difficult to decide whether a finger is conic tending toward square or just the opposite, that it is square tending toward conic. For the time being, judge only the very tips because the first step is to determine the general type classification.

Remember if Conic is in the majority, the emotional, idealistic quality is uppermost. If the Square predominates, materialism is the major qualification. If Spatulate, then activity is the motivating force. If Pointed, the psychic, intuitive instinct prevails.

D'Arpentigny, an early authority on the analysis of hands, said, "The intelligence which is revealed by a mixed hand is one which partakes of the nature of the intelligences attached to each of the forms represented."

FINGER COMBINATIONS

Whatever the combination of fingers, it represents the persons ideas and purposes. The latter may change from time to time, but certainly it shows adaptability to interests and surroundings.

There will be several talents plus the desire

The Mixed Hand

to excel in all. This is the problem that must be overcome. It is wiser to choose one strong interest toward an occupation. If time and strength permit, a second interest could be followed but only if it does not interfere with the main project. There are exceptions where, for instance, a good singer may also have acting ability. Then it is certainly advisable to proceed with the study for the stage because it could mean greater success and more remuneration.

Having checked the types of fingers, study the shape of the palm more closely. If the mixed fingers are on a square hand, add practicality. If they are combined with a spatulate palm, add a dynamic energy. If the spatulate is wider at the top of the palm, where it is joined with the fingers, the person should be actively engaged in the "public eye," where one is in direct contact with people. If the wider part of the palm is at the bottom where it is joined with the wrist, physical activities that embrace travel, such as employment in navigation, aviation, overland businesses. Both of these types like to investigate or explore things or places.

Mixed fingers with the firm rectangular palm of the Philosophic type will lend great variety, but can confuse the owner of these hands inasmuch as the knotty joints demand mental and material order in everything undertaken. It is easy to see that too many orderly, precise tasks would be too much of a burden.

SELECTIVITY OF THE PHILOSOPHICAL HAND

Since Philosophical Hands belong to the people who like to form their own opinions and make their own decisions, the mixed qualifications increase their amount of study and analysis. All of this requires more and more time, but only they, themselves, can select the project they wish to engage in, or effect a pattern of living that will best suit their abilities.

This Philosophical combination has one great asset which is adaptability, so they can work out their problems to better their lot in life.

Mixed Hands can easily fall into the category so often quoted "Jack of all trades, master of none" so it behooves the many owners of such hands to be satisfied with less interests and strive toward precision and perfection in just one trade, profession or occupation.

The latter includes the homemaker who may want to do too many things or retain too many interests outside the homelife. Being a mother or a wife can be a full time job and a wonderful life of gratification. Happy and well cared for children and a tidy attractive home create happiness and enduring love and kindliness.

9
THE
FINGERS

In addition to the traits shown by the shapes of the fingers, there are other finger features which form a distinct personality index. Length of fingers is a highly important factor.

Fingers are Long, Short, or Medium. Their length is determined by measuring from the very tip end of the second finger to the center point of the knuckle. You can see the knuckle clearly by bending the straightened finger slightly.

Now turn the hand over and measure up from the first ring of the bracelet (or the rascette) to the base of the second finger. This is exactly where the finger is joined to the palm. When the finger measurement is no longer than the palm it is considered a Long finger. When equal in length it is called Medium. When shorter than the palm, it is a Short finger.

The second finger is normally the longest finger of the hand.

Short fingers dislike detail. Long fingers prefer detail but may get side-tracked with too much love of detail.

Short fingers with Conical tips show an aptitude for the fine arts.

Short fingers with Spatulate tips dislike everything with detail. They love sports and enjoy participating in them.

Short fingers with Square tips react well to routine work or regimentation.

Short fingers with pointed tips are rarely found but do exist. They indicate a person who is inclined to be lazy and self-indulgent.

Long fingers with Conic tips have a quick perception of ideas and a love for details. Such finger types are found among artists, musicians, composers, actors and writers.

Long fingers with Spatulate tips never tire of outdoor sports. Usually like change of surroundings. Often they are witty.

Long fingers with Square tips indicate the ability to perform the everyday practical work. They range from domestic work to the highest business post. This variance depends upon a difference in thumb and line formations which will be described later in the book.

Long fingers with pointed tips are the sign of

The Fingers

Pointed

Conical

Square

Spatulate

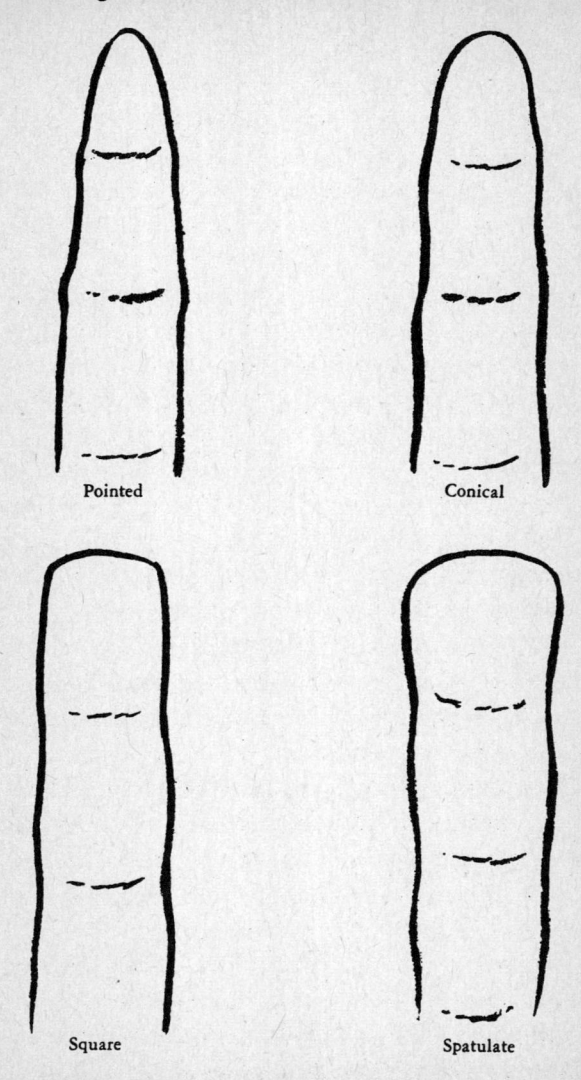

Four Types of Fingers

the psychic temperament with highly imaginative ideals.

Medium fingers are considered ideal. That is they coincide with the lines and mounts of the hand thus producing a well balanced mind.

HOW TO CLASSIFY FINGERS

If you find the long finger to be more than one-half inch longer than the palm then it must be classed as a very long finger. Likewise if it is one-half inch shorter than the palm it then is classed as a very short finger.

The first and third fingers normally reach to the half-way mark of the first phalange of the second finger; the little finger should reach up to the bending mark of the first phalange of the third finger.

So you see that in the nomal hand the first and third fingers are of equal length.

Any finger that is shorter or longer than average has a varying value on the qualifications of that particular finger. This in turn affects the interpretation of the entire hand. When all fingers are either very long or very short the entire nature is affected.

EXTREME TYPES

Very long fingers indicate the fault-finder who might resort to cruelty. Whether it would be mental or physical would depend on the type hand and its particular development. If it is a

The Fingers

modest palm or a highly educated indication, then interpretation would tend toward criticism or a contradictory nature. If the fingers are thin, be careful. These are the cunning fingers.

Very short fingers show indifference toward conventionality. People with these fingers prefer a Bohemian sort of life.

These overlong and very short fingers show abnormal characteristics.

Crooked or twisted fingers show varying degrees of nervousness.

Fingers that bend back tend to be careless and extravagant.

Finger tips that are cushioned with a soft padded rising effect of the flesh indicate sensitivity. When the little pad lies close to the end of the finger it denotes tactlessness.

When the major part of the hand is strong and good with good headline and heart line then these faults can be modified.

Fingers that are knotted show an analytical trend. These "knots" mean that the joints are noticeable and look knotty. There are three classes.

a — Knot at first joint, between first and second phalange, indicates an analytical ability in ideas.

b — Knot at second joint, between second and third phalange indicates the desire for order in material things. This means tidiness of person and surroundings. Everything must

58   Key to Palmistry

Long Oval   Short Oval

Large Squared   Short Squared   Spatulate

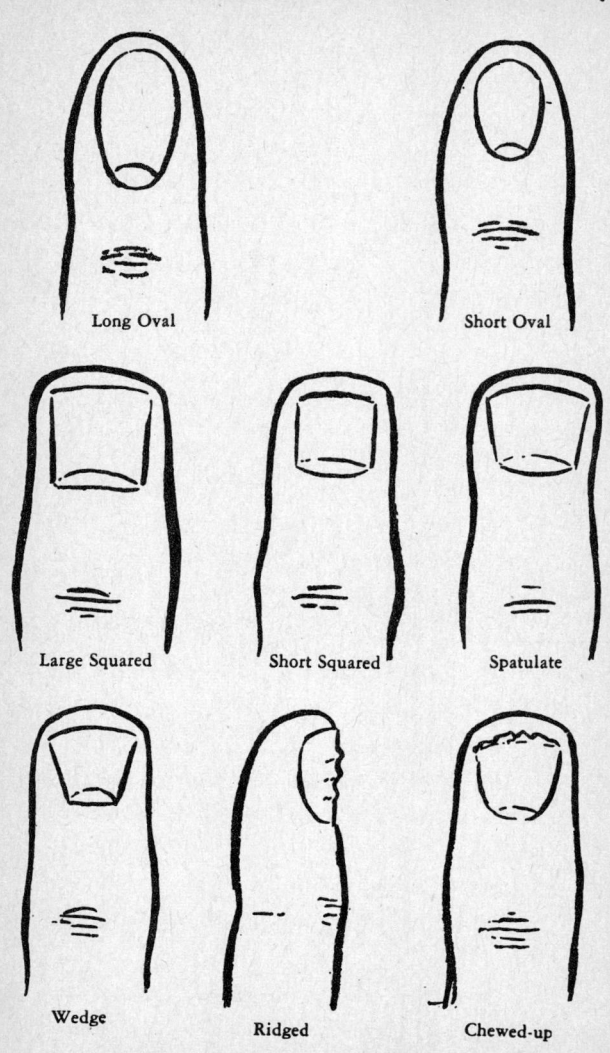

Wedge   Ridged   Chewed-up

Types of Finger Nails

The Fingers

be in its proper place.

c — Knots at both first and second joints which combine the meaning of the two knots "a" and "b." This places the owner of these hands "c" in the philosophical group.

Knotty fingers want to think things over methodically.

Smooth fingers like to act quickly, sometimes too impulsively. They also like quick answers.

FINGER-NAILS

Finger-nails should follow the general contour of the finger tip but very often they do not. They may be any one of the following:

The Long oval which follows the pattern of the well shaped conic finger.

The Short oval can be on long or short fingers but lends a critical slant to the temperament.

The Large squared imply carefulness about personal appearance.

The Short squared with oval base has a critical sense of humor.

The Short squared or spatulate turns to irony or revenge.

The Wedge indicates a nature that is too sensitive.

The Ridged and Fluted show a need for relaxation caused by strain.

The Chewed-up shows nervousness and shyness resulting from some form of nervousness.

10
THE
THUMB

The Thumb is the key to the entire secret of the hand. It is very revealing, just at a glance, because it determines the amount of will power and reasoning ability that controls and guides the entire life of the individual.

The Thumb consists of three parts, namely:

THE PHALANGES OF THE THUMB

The First Phalange has the thumb nail. This section denotes the amount of will power. The second section is called The Second Phalange which denotes the amount of reasoning ability. The third section lies in the palm of the hand and will be explained under the title of Mounts. For the moment to round out the basic thumb interpretation, this third section represents the amount of love and emotion that accompanies the will power and reasoning ability in each individual life.

MEASUREMENT OF THE THUMB

The measurement of the thumb is taken by placing the hand, palm down, on a flat surface. Hold the fingers and thumb together. Here the thumb lies against the first finger. If the tip of the thumb reaches to one-quarter of an inch of the lower joint of that finger or to the very line of the joint, it can be classed as a normal, average thumb. If the thumb is shorter than this measurement, it is classed as a long thumb. It represents good usage of intellectual powers.

Any thumb that extends more than a quarter of an inch beyond the markings of the lower joint of the first finger is considered as a very long thumb. Here there is a tendency to supersede anyone else.

While the hand is being checked for length of thumb it is necessary to look at the angle at which the thumb will open when separated from the fingers. Spread the thumb as far away from the first finger as it will go without forcing it.

THE THUMB ANGLE

The Thumb Angle is the name given to the

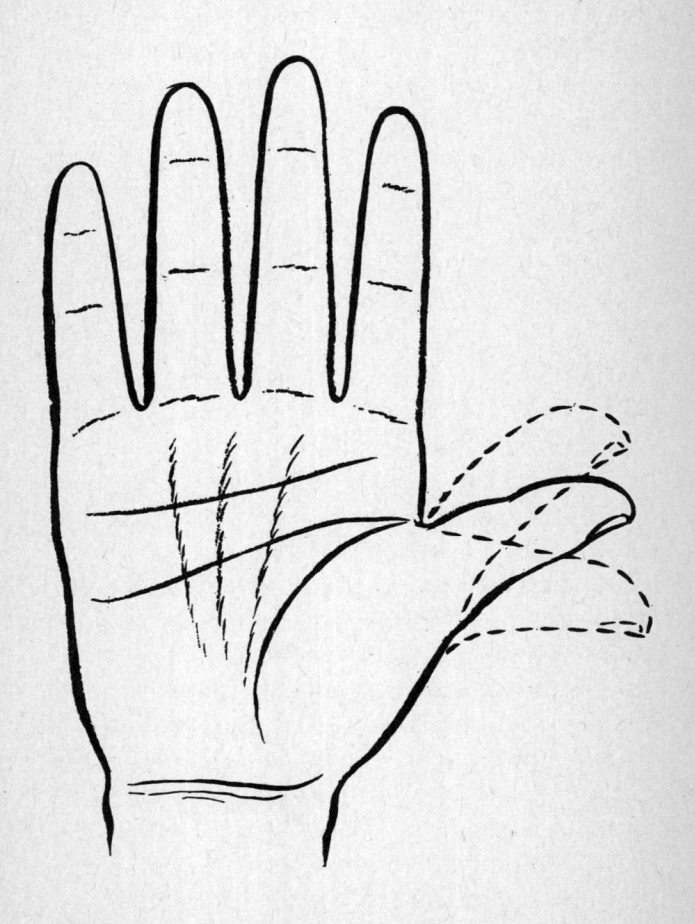

The Thumb

The Thumb

distance between thumb and finger. If the thumb lies open at right angles, it shows a desire to be an extremist, a love of show. These people like an audience. It is to be found among all classes of people, from the theatrical performer, the public speaker, the artist down the long list of occupations and professions and this includes housewives. This thumb is the sign of the extrovert.

If the thumb lies close to the fingers, this is the sign of a secretive nature.

The thumb that lies midway between these two extremes has the ideal Thumb Angle. If this same thumb is firm and long, then it is on the way to being considered a good thumb.

LENGTH OF THUMBS

Short thumbs are good too if they have the ideal Thumb Angle and sufficient firmness, but their interests are mainly concerned with the home, family or their closest friends, and the problems that arise from these sources.

The ideal thumb must have an equal amount of will power, which is represented by the first phalange, and logic, or reasoning ability, which is represented by the second phalange. If will power overbalances logic, it is easy to understand that the individual has a tremendous drive but lacks the correct amount of reasoning power to make a complete success.

Should the second phalange be much longer

The Thumb

than the first, the individual reasons out everything to the point of exactness, but lacks the will power to carry out the plan.

People with very short thumbs go from one extreme to another.

VARIATIONS OF THUMBS

Thick thumbs indicate bluntness. Frequently this is due to impatience. If the thumb is also broad it amounts to stubbornness.

If the thumb is stiff, then there is a certain fearfulness which causes secretiveness.

The thin thumb represents artistic tastes. Surroundings and friends must have a degree of refinement equal or better than their own.

A thumb that is very flexible is the mark of the person who is too generous. If in addition to this the fingers fall well apart, then it means the spender without thought for the future. It is an independent nature.

THUMB TIPS

The long thumb with a conic tip shows an artistic nature. A short one may be lazy or indifferent to family and friends.

The long spatulate thumb must curb the desire to strike out for self alone. The energetic urge should be developed with a group of people who have similar interests. The short spatulate thumb adds inpetuousness. This individual will worry and fret no matter what the undertaking.

The long square thumb seeks justice in everything. The short one is indecisive because of the desire to hold fast to all friends and does not want enemies.

COMBINATION OF THUMB AND FINGERS

Now by combining the meaning of the thumb and fingers, you can reach a better interpretation.

Take for instance the long thumb with a good balance of will power and reasoning ability plus the conic tip. Add to this long smooth fingers with conic tips. Here you have a person capable of methodically working out details. The conic thumb and fingers place this person in the realm of the artistic. The particular occupation would depend upon other features of the palm which are explained as this book proceeds. Here you would note if all fingers are normal in length.

The short conic thumb with conic fingers, all of which are well balanced would fall into the same category—the artistic—but here they would have to be idealistic to please the owner of such hands. They want things much faster than their long-fingered brothers.

Remember that squareness adds practicality; that the spatulate means activity; that the pointed is the extremist for perfection in mysticism, new thought ideas, philosophy or religion.

This is how you start to weave the story of each hand.

11
THE
MOUNTS

The Mounts of the hand are the fleshy areas that make up the entire surface of the palm. There are eight Mounts altogether. They are named respectively, Jupiter, Saturn, Apollo, Mercury, Upper Mars, Luna, Venus and Lower Mars. Look at the illustration of the Mounts of the Hand to check the location of each one.

PLACEMENT OF THE MOUNTS

You will see that the Mount of Jupiter lies directly beneath the Jupiterian, or first finger. The Mount of Saturn is beneath the second or Saturnian finger. The Mount of Apollo in turn is beneath the third, or finger of Apollo. Also the Mount of Mercury lies beneath the

Mercurian finger. All four of these mounts are situated on the upper part of the palm.

The lower part of the palm has the Mount of Luna on the lower outside section, while the lower right section below the thumb is called the Mount of Venus.

Between the Mount of Venus and the Mount of Jupiter is the area which is called Lower Mars. Upper Mars lies on the opposite side of the palm between the Mount of Luna and the Mount of Mercury.

THE APPEARANCE OF THE MOUNTS

The Mounts are so called because they appear as slight elevations. Usually several are noticeably higher than the others. If one or more are unusually high, the qualities of these mounts will influence the subject more than any of the other mounts. If only one mount is well developed, the person would be classed purely as that type. If no mount is developed, that person will have no particular flair.

The well developed mount has its highest spot in the center. This makes it the perfect formation. If also the texture markings called whorls form an apex in the center, this increases the characteristics of that particular mount.

If any mount is developed off center or is combined with another mount, it partakes of both but in lesser effect. For instance, if Mercury and Apollo, are joined, add up the qualifications

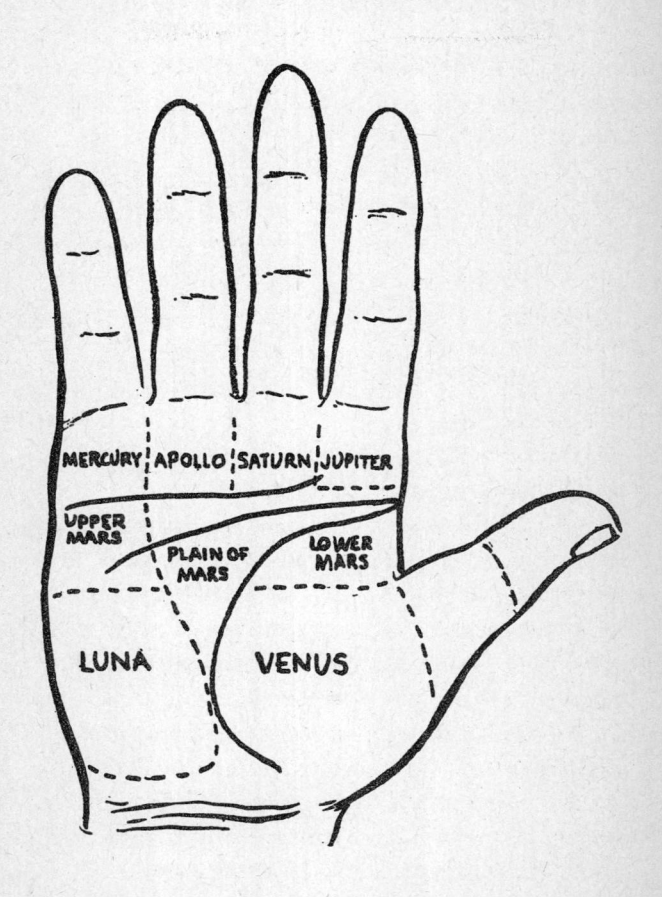

Diagram of Mounts

of each mount. If more rest on Mercury, then the person would have more Mercurian traits.

INTERPRETATION OF THE MOUNTS

Now for the interpretation of the mounts themselves.

Remember that no hasty conclusions can be drawn about any of the mounts without first considering the fingers. If perchance Jupiter happens to be the most prominently developed mount and the finger of Jupiter—the first finger directly above the mount—is excessively long, that person will belong to the exaggerated type of Jupiterian.

Always check the fingers with the mounts; then proceed. When the mount is developed in any part of the area other than the center, it is considered a displacement. This lessens the quality of the mount.

When it is normal, it is at its best. When it is abnormal it becomes a defect which can mean a vice of some sort. When completely absent, that particular mount has no evaluation.

The mounts should be firm but not hard. If they are soft it implies indolence or negligence. The person may have abilities but does not bother to develop them. If all the mounts are flat and hard, the person is likely to be very energetic.

The general meaning of each mount now follows.

12
THE
MOUNT OF
JUPITER

The Mount of Jupiter is essentially significant of pride. This shows itself in numerous degrees. In its best form it is indicative of ambition. If the highest part of the mount is close to the finger it means a belief in self, one who is not afraid to follow his or her own convictions or ideas. If the mount is heavier toward the area near the Saturn section, then the person suffers from self-consciousness. If the development lies at the bottom of the area there is pride of ownership. When the mount is lacking there is no respect for anybody or anything. An overdeveloped mount shows vanity, egotism, or a desire to rule or tower over everything.

The Mount of Jupiter is essential to success

and happiness, so it is present in varying degrees in all hands of successful people.

With pointed fingers, Jupiterians maintain very high religious ideals. They may be narrow minded about their own religion to the extent that they become intolerant of other religions. They will however be devoted to their own faith and follow the teachings devotedly.

Conical fingers add pride. This is evident with artists, singers, writers, and so on. They take pride in their work. They become meticulous and work ardently because they would be ashamed of anything that would not produce enthusiastic plaudits for their work.

Square fingers are proud of each days accomplishment. They may be artisans or craftsmen who work for a company or they may be following a small hobby that gives them an outlet for self-expression. This productivity shows pride in each days progress.

Spatulate fingers with the strong mount of Jupiter seek large or great enterprises. In this they take pride. They must be actively engaged to consume their energetic urge. They have the right to be proud. They make good leaders of industry. They become whirl-wind operators.

13
THE MOUNT OF SATURN

The Mount of Saturn, located just below the second finger, has always been the one mount that brings sadness, a love of solitude or a tendency toward morbidness. The latter quality is usually significant when the mount is excessively developed. When the mount is missing there is absolute indifference toward the feelings of others.

If the mount is higher near the base of the finger this intensifies the person's love for solitude. These people are usually very shy. If the apex lies close to the mount of Jupiter it represents sheer delight in morbidness. When closer to Apollo, the area under the third finger, there is an appreciation of sacred or somber music. If located at the base of the area there is always a feeling of worry or anxiety for the family or loved ones.

These people are very serious about everything they do. When the development is normal they are earnest serious workers. Many of them are to be found in church work, agriculture, husbandry or any of the occupations where they can find happiness through solitude.

Most musicians have a partial development of the Mount of Saturn. The heavier it is, the more will be the inclination toward classical music.

If the fingers are sharply conical there is a great appreciation for poetry that speaks of sadness or that has a serious story.

14
THE
MOUNT OF
APOLLO

The Mount of Apollo is also called the Mount of the Sun, after which it was named. It signifies a love for the artistic, for all that is beautiful. When it is an overall general development it indicates an appreciation for all of the arts even though the person may not be actively engaged in any one of them. They can see beauty in music, architecture, paintings, the countryside, everything that is artistic.

When the mount is excessive, you will find a poseur, a person who likes to pretend to know more about art or music than he or she really does.

Every one with creative and artistic talent has some form of development of this mount. If Apollo combines with Saturn, the temperament will be unpredictable. If, however, it combines with or is heavier near Mercury, which is under the little finger, then the temperament will be light, cheery and jovial.

Pointed fingers make dreamers of these people. Conical fingers add the talent for writing, composing or the quest for creative beauty in one form or another.

Square fingers add practicality. Many successful men and women in this group of professions have square fingers. The Spatulate group may be a little erratic but they are very original.

The lack of this Mount of Appollo is sad because these people have no appreciation for beauty. Some may be clever but at best can only be copyists.

15
THE MOUNT OF MERCURY

The Mount of Mercury is situated under the fourth or Mercurian finger. Named after Mercury, the god of commerce, this area represents the quickness of the mind. It also represents the channel of achievement.

When the mount is heavily padded there is a mind with quick perception. It denotes a person with the ability to change quickly from one idea to another, able to rationalize easily. This in turn produces a fine business instinct. All Mercurians have a bouyant nature. This quality alone accounts for so many salesman. They are blessed with an ability to create excitement.

If this mount combines with the Mount of Apollo under the third finger then indeed you will find a person with a very sunny disposition and a cheerful outlook upon life and business generally.

When the mount is heavier at the side of the hand it means a good sense of humor. All comedians possess this formation.

If the mount is heavier toward the lower section it adds physical strength. Many soldiers and professional fighters are in this class.

It is fortunate to have this mount and absolutely necessary for financial success. Doctors, lawyers, scientists, artists, financiers, all who gain prominence have this area well developed.

16
THE
MOUNT OF
LUNA

The Mount of Luna, the sign of the Moon, is the indicator of the imaginative qualities. It occupies the lower outside area of the palm. Check the illustration of Mounts until you are familiar with this area.

A firm mount gives a practical application of the imagination. There is a desire for change of surroundings which brings about travel. There is a love for family, a good balance of ideas. These are the people who like to read good literature, hear fine music.

If the mount is soft it is the sure sign of a dreamer, one who is unpractical. If the mount is flabby the emotions turn to lust and unconventionalities.

If the development is on the upper section,

there is an excellent ability for music. It represents the desire for harmony. If heaviest on the lower section there is too much tendency toward the exotic. The imagination actually 'runs away' with the individual.

When the outside of the area is rounded or extended there is a great love of water, a desire to travel. Explorers, navigators, seamen, fishermen and innumerable others are really Lunarians. Writers of fiction and composers of highly imaginative music usually have this formation in combination with other mounts and markings.

When the mount is absent, you find a very cold and unsympathetic nature. These people are disinterested in everything except themselves.

17
THE MOUNT OF VENUS

The Mount of Venus, named for the Goddess of Love, designates the capacity for love, passion, friendship and sympathy. It is the area at the base of the thumb and occupies the largest area of all the mounts. It is the indicator of health, strength and happiness.

This area completely surrounds the thumb. It should be well padded and firm. This indicates a strong and healthy person. It represents a sympathetic nature, an understanding for the welfare and happiness of others. With it goes an affectionate loving disposition and a fair amount of passion. This in turn produces a happy home and a well rounded life.

When the lower part of the thumb formation looks angular there is ability for rhythm. This means a definite interest in music or dancing. Often it combines both talents.

If this area is flat there is a lack of sympathy. This is the person who is hard in business and usually indifferent in the home.

If the fullest development is at the top section of the mount, it means deep affection for the family. Both men and women will be willing to sacrifice anything for the family. Many a mother and father has this type of area.

When the fullest section lies close to the arc line—(known as the Life Line which surrounds this area) it is indicative of intense sexual desires. The flesh looks as though it is bulging along side the line close to the center of the palm.

18
THE MOUNTS OF MARS

The Mount of Upper Mars lies on the percussion, the outside edge section of the palm, between Mercury and Luna. It is called Upper Mars because it is normally situated above the Head Line.

This is the sign of the fighting spirit, one that will resist wrong-doing. In its best form the owner of this area has courage and dignity. He or she will never let things get out of control. They are consistent and persistent. Well formed, it adds the ability to command either in the battlefield or in the courtroom. Most brilliant people have a good share of the qualifications of this mount.

Underdeveloped the opposite is true. There will be no forcefulness. A fear complex may be existent. When the mount is very high, there is the power of great endurance physically. If the area is rounded out and heavier toward the section of Luna there will be the gift of foresight. These people have good judgment. They appear to be slow in making decisions but it is only because they wish to weight the pro and con of every problem or project which they undertake.

The heavier development toward the Mercurian area shows endurance only for the sake of the family. Nothing else seems to matter. These are the sons and daughters who will do no wrong lest it offend their parents. Parents may go to extremes rather than interfere with the happiness of their children.

THE MOUNT OF LOWER MARS

The Mount of Lower Mars is actually the very upper section of the Mount of Venus. It is just inside the Life Line which marks off the Venus area. This means that Lower Mars is actually between the area of Jupiter and Venus.

Lower Mars is also the sign of the fighter. It differs from Upper Mars in that it actually adds the act of fighting physically. It is courageous, but martial. It makes the fighting soldier, the fighter in the boxing and wrestling arena. It also produces any quarrelsome person who turns pugnacious. The balanced mount is to be found in a person of great physical strength.

The Mounts of Mars

Spatulate fingers combined with this mount produce a nature that withstands pain. This same person will also be fearless.

Square fingers indicate great patience in working out militant problems.

Conical fingers show a stoical spirit like so many of the Chinese and the Indians. They inure themselves when under the stress of great pain.

Pointed fingers add resignation. In this group are the martyrs for church or country.

When over developed there is the spirit of cruelty. It can be active or passive but nevertheless it is there.

When the Mount of Lower Mars is missing the palm seems hollow in this portion. This is the sensitive person. One who is afraid to make a move. It is a fear of physical pain. Cowards lack this mount.

THE PLAIN OF MARS

The Plain of Mars is the center of the palm which is not actually included with any of the mounts.

If the Plain is gently hollowed it is normal. This shows a good balance with the other parts of the palm. The temperament is even. The person has good mental control.

Should the Plain be level there is lack of control. It means impetuosity, too much spirit, too daring when there is no such need.

The Plain that is very hollow is not good. It denotes a timid person, one who will not take his own part in an argument. There is a fear of lack of finance, fear of the future, coupled with a general moroseness and feeling of futility.

19
SPECIAL MARKINGS ON THE PALM

There are special signs or markings on the palms that are not necessarily on the lines. They are usually on one of the Mounts or in the Plain of Mars. When they touch a line they then have a special bearing on the interpretation of the line itself.

THE CIRCLE

The Circle is seldom seen but it heralds a brilliant success when it appears on the Mount of Apollo. If it is on the Mount of Luna it warns about danger that may come from water. This may be either in or on or over water. It covers a wide range of possibilities because it involves all modes of traveling, boating and swimming. A Circle on the Head Line is considered to mean an accident to an eye but there must be another circle or a sharp break on the Life Line.

THE GRILLE

The Grille is a mesh of cross lines that actually look like grillework. It is a sign of misfortune. Traditionally the readings follow a pattern of a temperament that gets out of control. On the Mount of Jupiter that is developed it indicates a tyrranical spirit. If the mount is low, then the person leans toward superstition. On Saturn it forbodes ill luck. If it is on a very bad hand, then imprisonment may ensue. On Apollo, extreme conceit. On Mercury, a thieving or swindling streak. On Mars, murderous intent that could result in death. On Luna, if the Grille is very large it means inconstancy. If only on the upper section the health needs continual check-up. If the Grille is not too large but heavy with lines it means morbidness.

STARS

Stars are really shockers. They are omens of great success or misfortune. On Jupiter and Apollo a Star means wealth that may come unexpectedly. Saturn is less fortunate. Here the Star brings death by violence. On Mercury, it means financial success without much effort. On

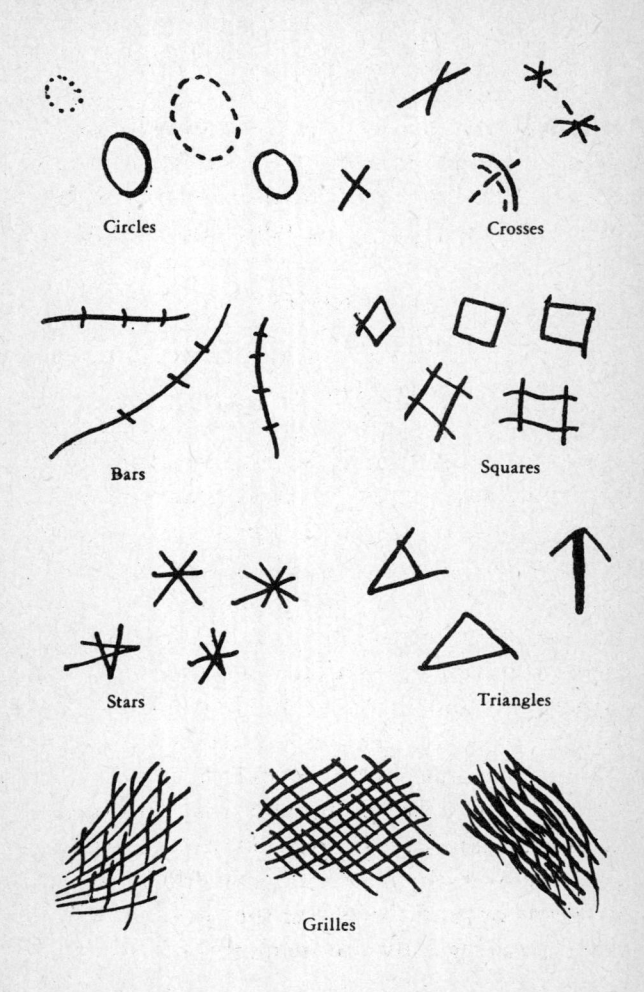

Special Markings on the Palm 89

Circles

Crosses

Bars

Squares

Stars

Triangles

Grilles

Special Markings

the Mount of Venus, a brilliant marriage produces unexpected happiness and wealth. Luna threatens danger from drowning. A Star on the Head, Heart or Life lines threatens illness. If the Line of Apollo ends on the Mount of Apollo with a Star directly on it, then there will be a brilliant success bringing fame and money.

CROSSES

Crosses vary in size and formation. They can be large or small. The only place where they are favorable is on the Mount of Jupiter. Here it means a marriage or an alliance that centers the emotions on one particular way of living. This includes a tie with the church or some order where the highest and purest ideal is attained. A Cross on the Mount of Venus also signifies a union for love but in this case it is seldom a happy situation. A Cross that has a Square around it is a good marking. The Square preserves the person from misfortune. On all the other Mounts and on all lines the Cross brings disappointment and misfortune. It is translated in proportion to the size and placement on the palm. Whenever a strong line proceeds beyond the Cross, the problem will be solved leaving only the memory of it.

BAR LINES

Bar Lines are little sharp lines that cross the

Special Markings on the Palm

main lines. These are obstacles. For instance on Line of Affection this means a separation from a close friend or loved one. On the Life Line the same thing applies but it involves the family too. On the line of Mercury it would apply to a business associate.

SQUARES

Squares can be closed or open. Either way they are good because they promise protection. No matter what danger is marked on the hand, if it has a square around it or near it, the person escapes the warning of danger or recovers from the misfortune received.

TRIANGLES

Triangles are really lucky markings. They always brings success. Translate them in relation to the mounts or lines where they happen to be placed. They are the mark of a brilliant intelligence.

20
THE
LINES
OF THE PALM

The Lines of the Palm can be likened to a map. They point the way of living by means of traditional interpretations. There are often many lines. Some are long, some are short. To begin, one must first learn the names and placement of the long major lines.

THE MAJOR LINES

There are three lines which every normal being must have in the palm of the hands. They are called the Line of Heart, the Line of Head and the Line of Life. They represent respectively the emotional, mental and physical world of each person. These lines start on the thumb side of the palm and run toward the percussion side.

THE THREE NECESSARY LINES

The lines of each pair of hands differ but these three lines must be there in some form. The best lines are unbroken and in a clear continuous form. This is the ideal, but there are few lives that have ever been perfect so it is logical that there are many variations of lines.

Study the illustration for the placement of the lines. Then look for them in your own hands. Do not try to check the small lines when you start. They depend upon the main lines, so the long main lines are important for first study and observation.

OTHER MAJOR LINES

The next three long lines are not so essential, yet are rich in their interpretations, whenever they appear. These lines are called:

The Line of Fate, or Line of Saturn, which represents your way of living, such as adaptability to home surroundings and to some degree the shaping of a career.

The Line of the Sun, or Line of Apollo, has to do with success, which also is inclusive of a career, but particularly in choice of a field or profession.

The Line of Mercury, or Line of the Liver, particularly covers health and finances.

All three of these lines start at the base of the palm and run upward toward the fingers of

The Lines of the Palm

Saturn, Apollo and Mercury respectively.

Many hands possess only one of these lines, so in such cases the emphasis is on that one phase. That is a person may be a home lover, or wedded to his chosen work, or strictly concerned with finance, as the case may be.

Some hands show two of these lines, signifying a double interest, or ability in both phases that are represented.

A few hands have all three lines, but these are quite rare. When they do appear, they may be significant of a powerfully overwhelming personality.

THE MINOR LINES

Now check the lesser lines. Above the Line of Heart lies the Girdle of Venus which increases the sensual nature of the Heart Line. Another line close to this area of sensitivity is the Ring of Saturn which means a morbid, overserious outlook on life.

Straight short lines on the percussion side of palm between the base of the little finger and the Heart Line are called the Affection Lines.

The Ring of Solomon is below the first finger forming an arc on the Mount of Jupiter. This is a mark of interest in the mystic or occult realm of thinking.

The Line of Mars is a "sister line" running parallel to and inside the Life Line.

The Cephalic Line runs parallel to the Line

of Mercury. It is also called the Via Lascivia. In solid form it increases any tendency toward a vice. In broken form it creates a desire to turn every idea into a money-making scheme.

The Line of Intuition is a curved line that in a solid form looks like a crescent.

RIGHT HANDED VS. LEFT HANDED

Not all of these lines are to be found in all hands; but you must know them to be able to read the palms. Also there may be more lines on one hand than on the other. By tradition it is customary to consider a difference in right and left handed people. If the person is right handed then the left hand indicates the talents and possible years of longevity. The right hand tells what has been done proportionately. Sometimes a person does a great deal more than the left hand predicts. With others it is the contrary.

For the left handed person the reading is the reverse, i.e., the right hand predicts and the left shows the progress.

THE RASCETTES

The Rascettes, also called Bracelet Lines are at the bend of the wrist. They corrobrate length of life as measured by the main lines.

The Rascettes, according to old tradition, can be studied as an indication of longevity. The

The Lines of the Palm

simple practice was to regard each bracelet line as representing 30 years of life, but there is little to confirm this mode of measurement.

True, many persons do have Rascettes that show two sharp, well-defined lines, with a third that is weaker or only partly complete. So it would be easy to rate these according to the old formula of 70 years—"three score and ten" as the allotted age of men.

Perhaps that is where the idea came from; but you will find many triple Rascettes—totalling 90 years!—and even some four-fold examples which would mean a ripe old 120 years. So the Rascettes can hardly be held reliable on that count.

There are other and more important ways of interpreting:

TIME MEASUREMENT BY LINES

The Life Line, first of all, has long been regarded as the key to a long life. But this too is a mistaken concept. What the Life Line does reveal is a person's status or what he may encounter at various phases of his life—if he lives that long.

Where the Life Line weakens or becomes broken, you can expect some weakness or a change, or perhaps an illness at that age, when attained. But the Life Line can fade entirely and life will still go on. Then, however, you may need the stamina that some other stronger

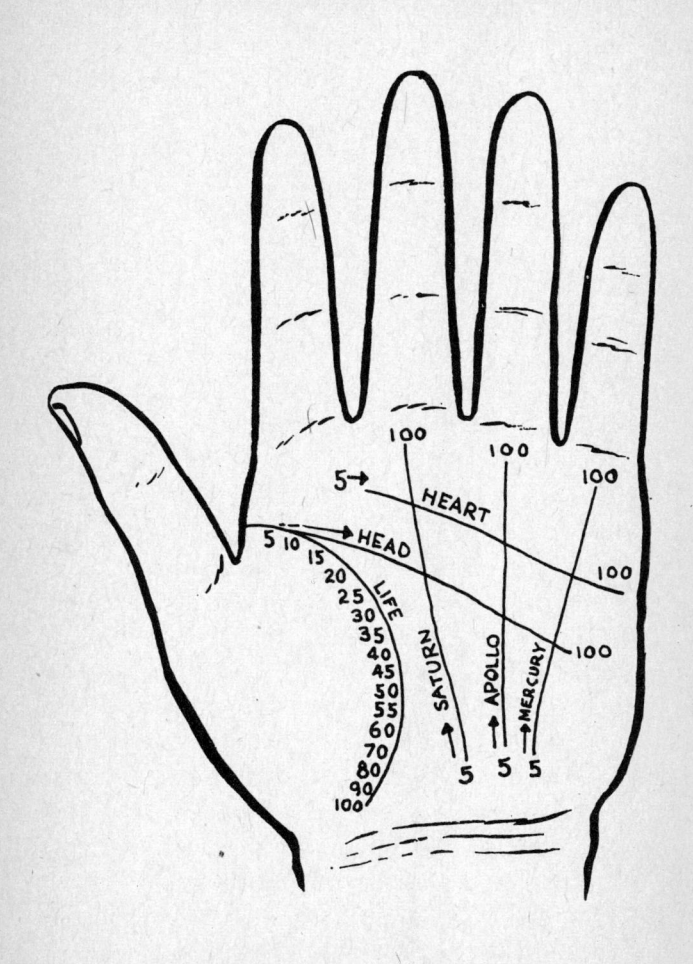

Measurement of Time

The Lines of the Palm

line might provide.

The age measurement on the Life Line is shown on the accompanying chart. By following around the arc formed by the line, gauging the age at places where odd markings or signs appear on the Life Line, you can estimate the age where these should take effect.

It takes years of experience to pinpoint the exact time so the novice must allow a few years one way or another for calculation. Also the early years need a little more spacing to estimate the passing of time, while the later years crowd into lesser and lesser space.

The Heart Line is measured from the inside of the hand to the outside edge, running from 5 to 100 years for a very long Heart Line. This follows the same as the Life Line and all other major lines, as far as measured spacing. If there is a special mark for instance on the Line of Life at approximately the "20" year space, then check on the Heart Line for corroboration. This might be a break in the line itself, or a dot, bar island, cross and so on. In this way you can determine if the mark pertains to the emotions which could change one's way of living or it might be something physical.

The Head Line is measured on a similar scale to the Heart Line. A long Head Line is needed to bolster a short Life Line. On the contrary a long Life Line with a short Head Line has little recourse for help from other lines. It may indicate a lessening of memory and other mental faculties with the increasing years.

The Fate Lines, namely Saturn, Apollo and Mercury are measured upward, starting at the base of the hand, near the Rascettes—which is their normal starting point. If any one of them starts above this place, then subtract the approximate distance to ascertain the correct age of beginning. In each case you can follow the growth of the individual in whatever occupation or career that may have been achieved. Remember that on the Line of Saturn the happy and helpful homemaker is very likely to have a strong line, which indicates a successful life. Branches from it may indicate interest in the careers of children or husband. Apollo and Mercury lines add exceptional abilities that turn to professional and financial groups. Breaks in any of these lines mean a change of circumstances. Whether for better or worse depends upon the physical and mental strength of the individual. This can be checked by studying the Life Line and the Head Line in both hands. Remember that a strong thumb that shows good drive and reasoning ability plus a strong Head Line can overcome almost anything.

12
THE APPEARANCE OF THE LINES

Lines should be free of any breaks or irregularities. They should be of the same depth and width for the entire length of each line.

Red lines indicate a healthy strong body with an active mind. There is a definite energetic desire to work and achieve a goal that will lead to success and happiness.

Very red lines tell of a temperament that is too fiery, too quick to be provoked or cause provocation.

Black or darkish lines represent sadness, moroseness and often a nature that can never be reached by love or friendship. This can be counteracted by a good Mount of Venus and a strong Heart Line.

Pale lines show lack of energy. Not sufficient vitality to carry out the possibilities offered by the lines themselves. Anyone with such pale lines should exert every effort to improve their physical condition.

Lines are the indicators of a tendency toward a condition or effect. Usually a bad effect or condition can be improved, however it is entirely up to the person who possesses the lines. Lines change from time to time. They can vanish completely or partially, so it is easy to understand how one can improve self and surroundings by knowing what lies in the reading of the palm.

FORMATIONS OF LINES

Where a second line runs very closely parallel to a main line it is called a sister line. This one serves as a booster or strengthens the main line. It also helps in case the main line is broken or irregular.

Broken lines are either clean cut breaks or they form an overlay. The latter acts as a continuation of the acting force of the line proper. It signifies a delay or temporary interference. This is considered a lucky break. If a main line has a clean sharp break without a sister line it is a serious matter. It needs serious consideration.

A Square covering the section of a broken line means protection at that particular time.

The Appearance of the Lines

Sister Lines

Forks

Frayed Lines

Clean Breaks

Tassels

Chains

Overlapping Breaks

Wavy

Islands

Square on
Broken Line

Branches
Ascending & Descending

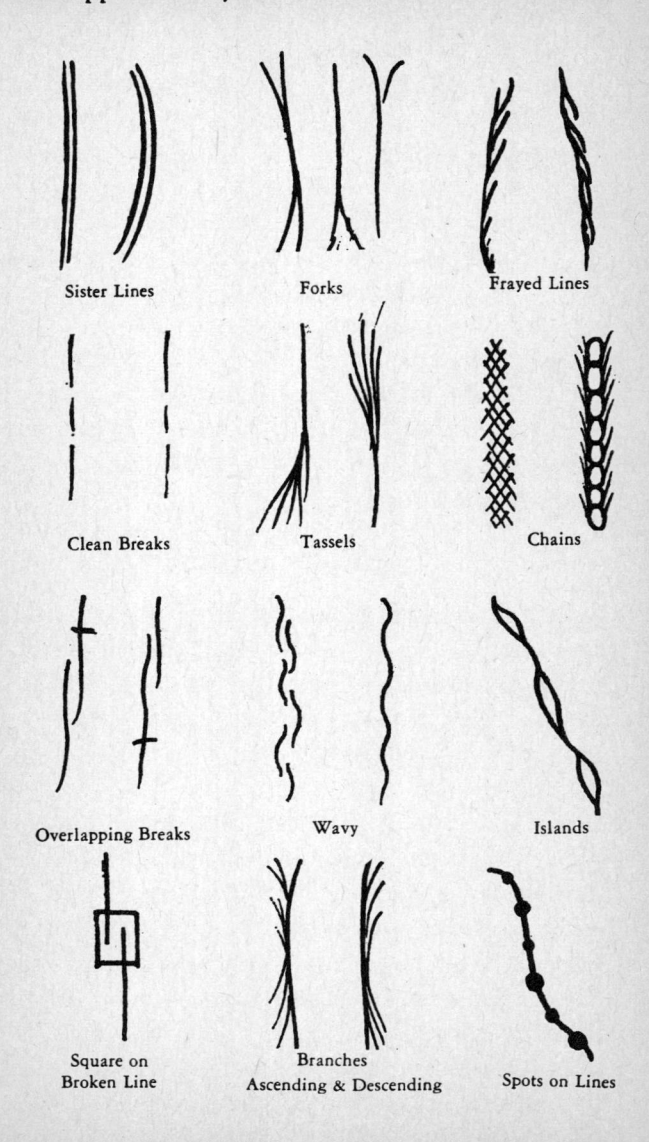

Spots on Lines

The Appearance of Lines

It is a mark of safety.

A two-tined fork on a main line is a strengthener with only one exception. If it be on the Life Line it diminishes the value. Physical strength weakens at this point. A three-tined fork triples the value.

A Tassel is a complete breakdown of the value of any line. Always a scattering of forces that pertain to the particular main line to which it is attached.

Wavy lines designate instability. Again this pertains only to particular line that it represents. If the Head Line happens to be wavy there would be mental weakness.

MEANINGS OF BRANCHES

Ascending branches are very helpful. They add impetus to one's ambition.

Descending Branches detract from the value of the main line to which they are attached.

When a branch springs from one line and then touches another there will be some amalgamation of the two main lines. The power robbed from the one line will also affect the other main line. If, for instance, a descending line starts from the Heart Line and ends on the Head Line, there would be some affair of the heart or some emotional strain that would affect the mental powers for some period of time.

Frayed lines are little tiny lines that produce

The Appearance of the Lines

a feathery appearance on a main line. This too is a weakening, a type of time-killing, time-wasting that never accomplishes anything outstanding.

MARKINGS ON LINES

Chains in any line are a defect wherever they occur. They indicate delicacy. On the Life Line it pertains to the physical condition. On the Heart Line it reaches the emotional state. In extreme cases it could apply to the heart itself or to a respiratory problem.

Islands are definite openings where a line looks as though it splits at one point and joins again after leaving a round or elongated space. They are to be found singly or in a series. Fortunately Islands are seldom found, but when they are, it means a serious study. They are not to be confused with the chained appearance of a line. The chain is a definite crossing of lines that have a link formation. An island signifies a physical problem that is accidental or self-imposed. The latter applies to emotions that are not under control. This can lead to a mental lapse or a breakdown. Each line bears its own interpretation for the island. An island on the Fate Line involves business as well as an emotional upheaval. These conditions last for the period of time indicated by the island itself. Time can be computed by the illustration on Time.

SPOTS AND THEIR SIGNIFICANCE

Spots on lines vary in size and color. They can be tiny or they can be the size of a pin head. They are signs of illness.

Black Spots on the Life Line are said to mean nervous ailments. Blue Spots threaten fever. White Spots, also on the Life Line, mean that one must protect the eyes.

Spots on the Heart Line mean depression caused by sadness.

Spots on the Head Line under Jupiter warn of tension. If the spot falls under Apollo, the ears are to be given special care.

When the hands are covered with many small lines that look like a maze of nondescript goings and comings it indicates a temperament inclined to worry over everything.

22
THE
HEART
LINE

STARTING POINTS

The normal Line of Heart starts from the Mount of Jupiter, drops to the base of the mount, then proceeds across the hand in a straight line to the percussion side of the palm. This is the ideal balance for a well proportioned life, one that is well controlled where emotions are concerned.

When the Line of Heart crosses the entire width of the palm starting from the thumb side, there is danger from excessive sex instincts causing an unbalanced emotional complex. If there is also a heavily padded Mount of Luna, jealously would be very evident.

If the line starts high on the bottom phalange

108   **Key to Palmistry**

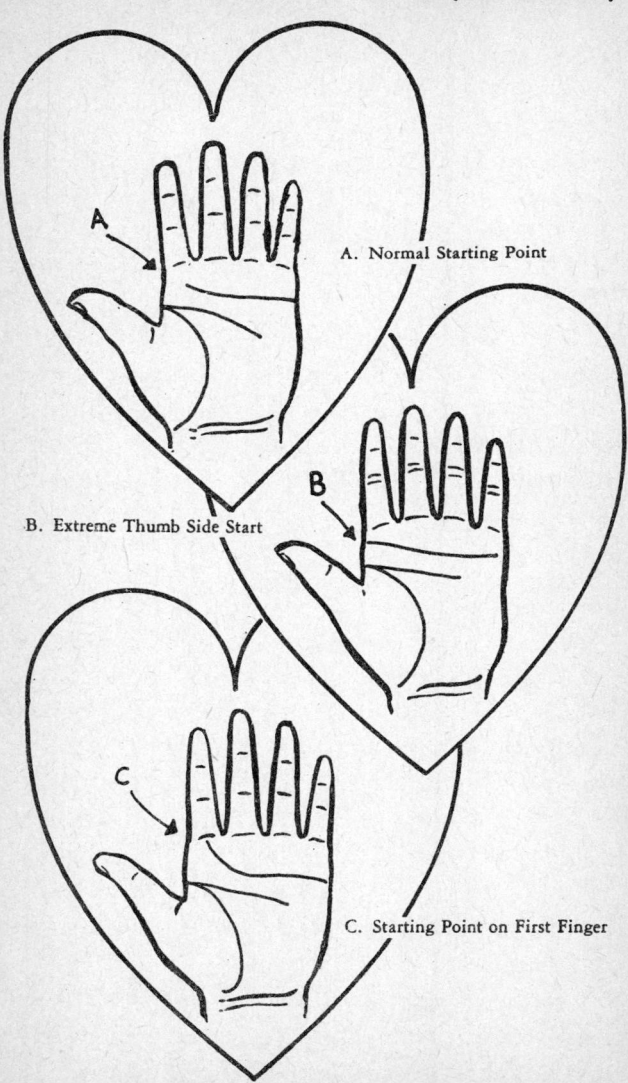

A. Normal Starting Point

B. Extreme Thumb Side Start

C. Starting Point on First Finger

Starting Points of Heart Lines

The Heart Line

of the first finger, intrigue and complications may cause the individual undue bitterness. This results because of too much trust, devotion and blind love for someone unworthy of such affection.

A Heart Line joined at the start to the Head and Life Lines warns of sudden danger that could be very serious.

If the line rises between Jupiter and Saturn, there will be an ideal love, one of deep devotion.

A forked beginning, with one prong on Jupiter and the other between Jupiter and Saturn means a desire for a happy home and a loving family life.

TERMINATIONS

A Line of Heart that curls around upward onto the Mount of Mercury means an inquiring mind. If it almost touches the little finger there will be a definite interest in all things pertaining to occultism.

A forked end shows a personal problem that could teminate in a separation. This would apply to marriage or to business, whichever the case might be. Long strong Head and Life Lines can counteract such a climax.

Chained formations are not helpful. They mean instability of the emotions. This usually means infidelity. When the Life Line is also chained or frayed, there is a physical weakness.

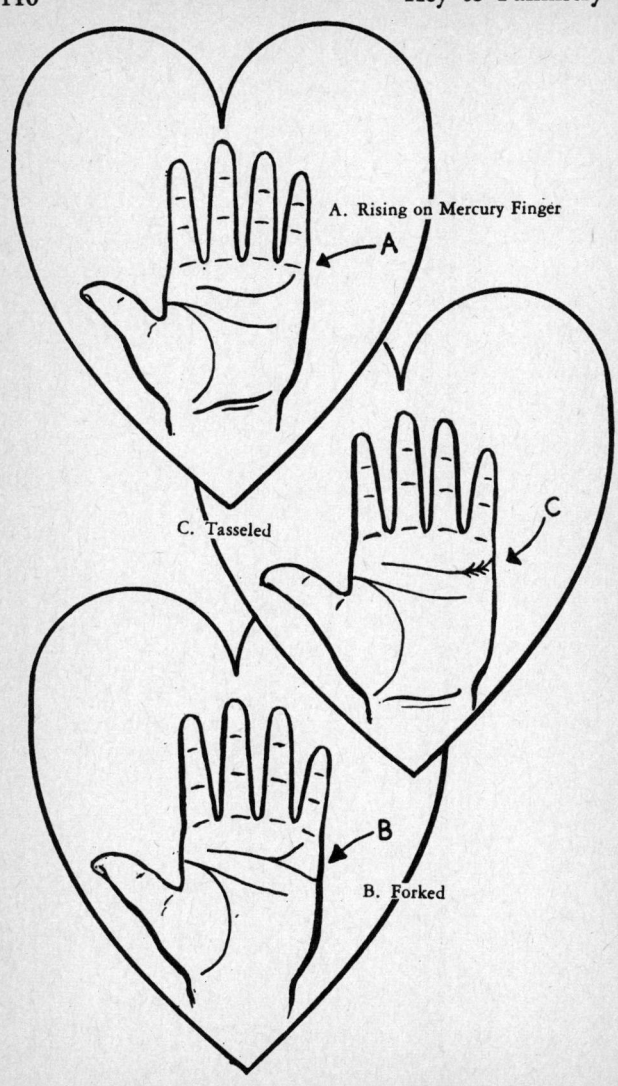

Termination of Heart Lines

The Heart Line

A tasseled ending is the mark of the flirt, a person who likes to have many amours. A very heavy or much marked tassel designates the philanderer.

Sometimes a double line or Sister Line runs parallel. This strengthens the good qualities of the Heart Line. If it is toward the end of the line, then there is exceptional physical strength and a deep emotional capacity for affection and love.

23
THE
HEAD
LINE

STARTING POINTS

The normal Line of Head is joined to the Life Line at its starting point. From there it rises gently for a little distance then drops as it proceeds across the palm. It should end somewhere on the Mount of Lower Mars but it does not go to the edge of the palm. This shows the well balanced mind, a person who is cautious without being critical, sensitive without being irritable.

The Line of Head that is separated from the Life Line just slightly indicates too much self confidence.

Widely separated it means a conceited nature, one that will go to extremes. Recklessness is the keynote for this type. With a short line,

A. Normal

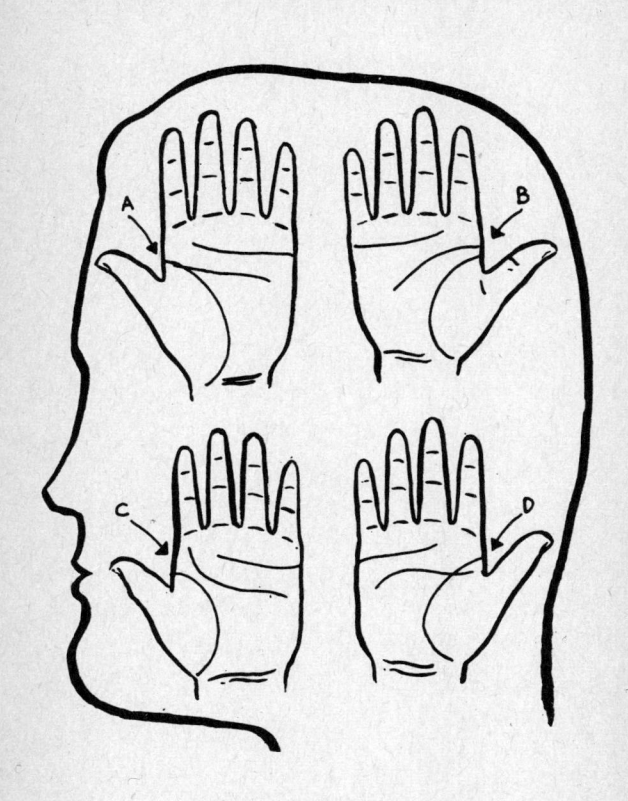

B. Separated

C. On Mount of Jupiter

D. Inside Lifeline

Starting Points of Head Lines

The Head Line

such a person would be the worst offender. A very long line adds a fine intellect but the individual must guard against tactlessness.

Rising on the Mount of Jupiter, there exists an unending ambition for success. Such people make good administrators.

Starting inside the Life Line on Upper Mars it produces a very sensitive, worrying nature, one that changes ideas constantly.

TERMINATIONS

The Head Line that terminates in a small fork under Mercury is an excellent one. It adds imaginative ability to a commercial mind. If one prong of the fork runs down on Luna, the imagination becomes too strong. There would have to be an outlet such as writing or music or travel. If the longer prong rises to the Mount of Mercury, there is a crafty ability for salesmanship or some equivalent in business.

The triple fork ending, sometimes called a trident, links a brilliant mind with talent and business acumen.

If the Line of Head stops abruptly under any one of the Mounts, every effort should be made to overcome the defects. Under Saturn it is traditionally translated as a fatal accident. Under Apollo, very little imaginative ability but very practical.

People with short headlines usually have ex-

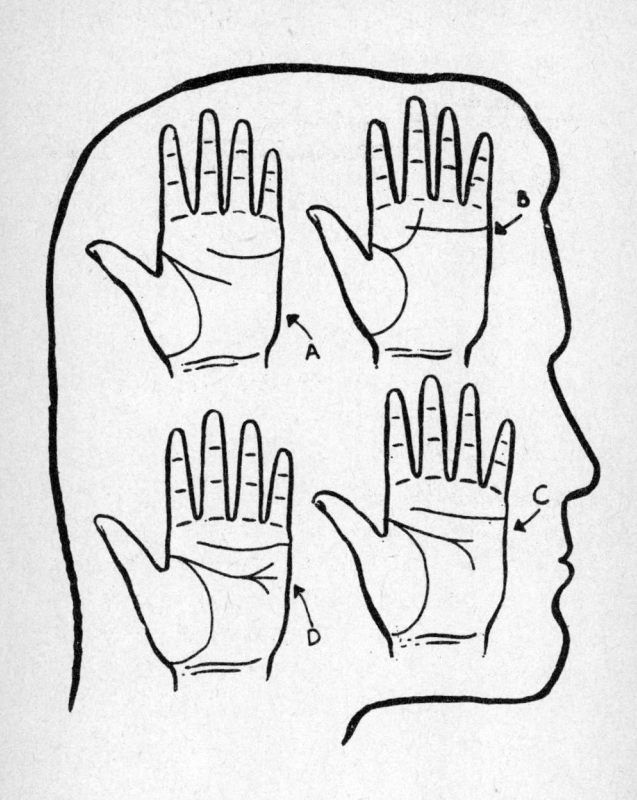

A. Abrupt   B. On Mount of Saturn

C. Forked   D. Trident

Terminations of Head Lines

cellent memories during their childhood and adolescent years.

If the Head Line runs straight across the hand, terminating on the percussion, the subject possesses an exceptional intellect, but is inclined to be selfish and secretive.

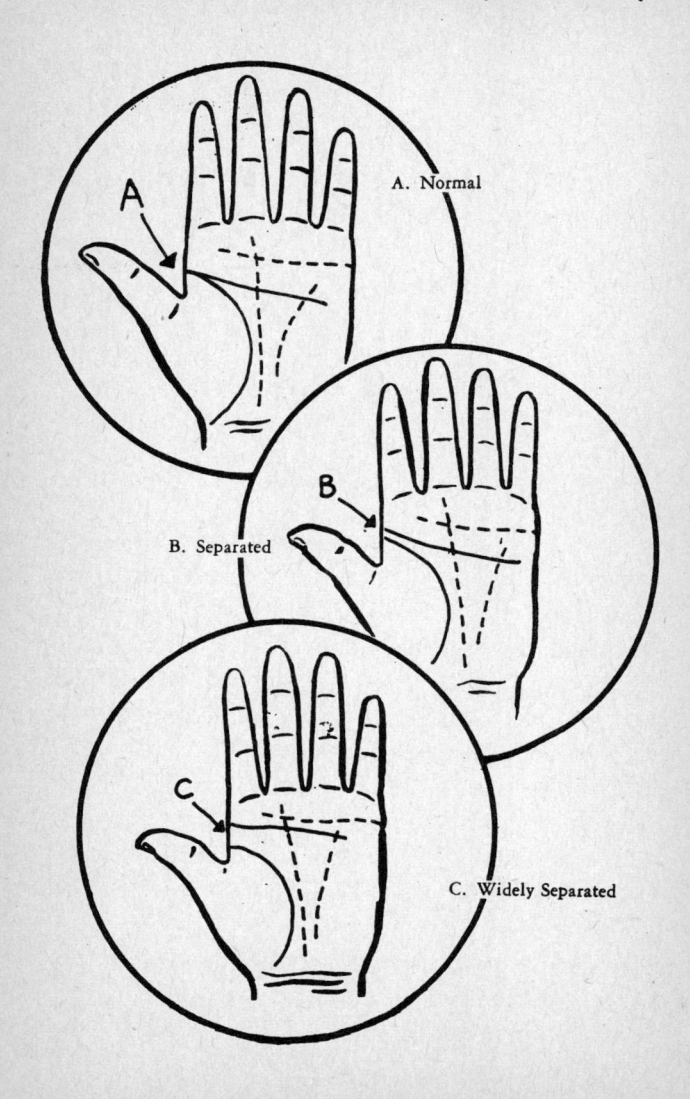

Starting Points of Life Lines

24
THE
LIFE
LINE

STARTING POINTS

The Line of Life normally starts with the Line of Head on the thumb side of the palm. In this form it signifies the beginning of a well balanced intelligent person who is or will be sensitive about all things personal, meaning self and family. There is also a reasonable appreciation for friends and acquaintances. What the individual does as life advances, must be read from the length and appearance of the lines.

Separation of these lines means lack of caution. The wider the separation the greater the recklessness.

A chained beginning means poor health in early childhood. As the line grows clear, the health improves.

120   **Key to Palmistry**

A. Abrupt—Short

B. Broken—Continuing

C. Forked

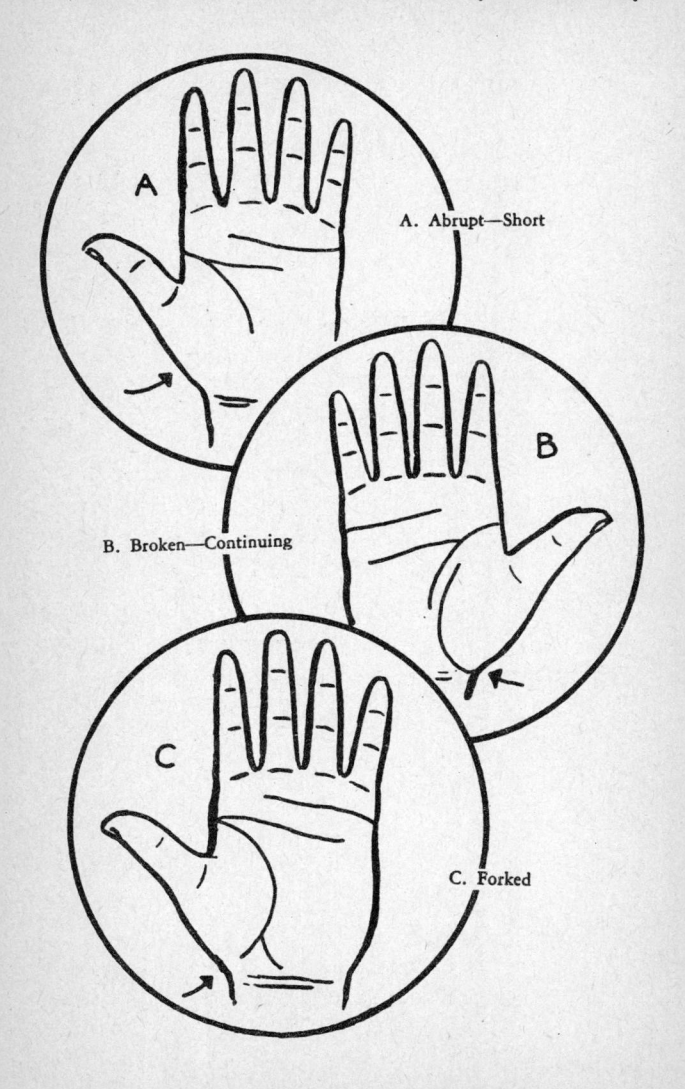

Endings of Life Lines

The Life Line

When the Life Line starts on the Mount of Jupiter there is a great ambition for the social standing of the family.

A branch to Jupiter means personal ambition for social recognition.

A curled start on the inside area of the Mount of Venus denotes inconstancy.

Crisscross lines at the start between the Life and Head Lines denote family problems that affect the financial status of the individual.

TERMINATIONS

Short, abrupt terminations of the Life Line have been traditionally interpreted to mean an early and sudden death. However, many hands with short life lines refute this translation. With long head lines or long fate lines there is a great chance for longevity. Such a short life line does mean a change of some sort, but it can apply to surroundings or occupation.

Lines that show breaks but continue in solid form indicate a recovery from an illness or from financial losses.

Forked Life Lines show a diminishing of physical strength. This is not usually fatal if steps are taken to avoid undue strain.

When a wide curve of the Life Line dips into the Plain of Mars, in the center of the palm, it shows a tremendous amount of physical endurance.

If the line ends on the Mount of Luna, the

individual has the choice of living in a country or place other than that of his birth.

A branch near the end of the Life Line that stretches over to the Mount of Luna adds restlessness and a desire to travel.

25
THE
FATE
LINES

STARTING POINTS OF THE LINE OF SATURN

The normal Line of Fate is the Line of Saturn. It starts close to the wrist but not touching the Rascettes, then proceeds in a straight line upward to the Mount of Saturn. This line is seen more frequently than the other two fate lines, namely the Line of Apollo and the Line of Mercury, hence it has been commonly called the only Fate Line. When it is found in the palm in its normal form it signifies a fair amount of wealth and great happiness.

Starting from the first bracelet of the Rascettes, the individual must take on financial responsibilities during the early years of life. This means either self support or assistance to the

124　　　　　　　　　　　　　　　　　Key to Palmistry

A. Normal

B. Touching Rascettes

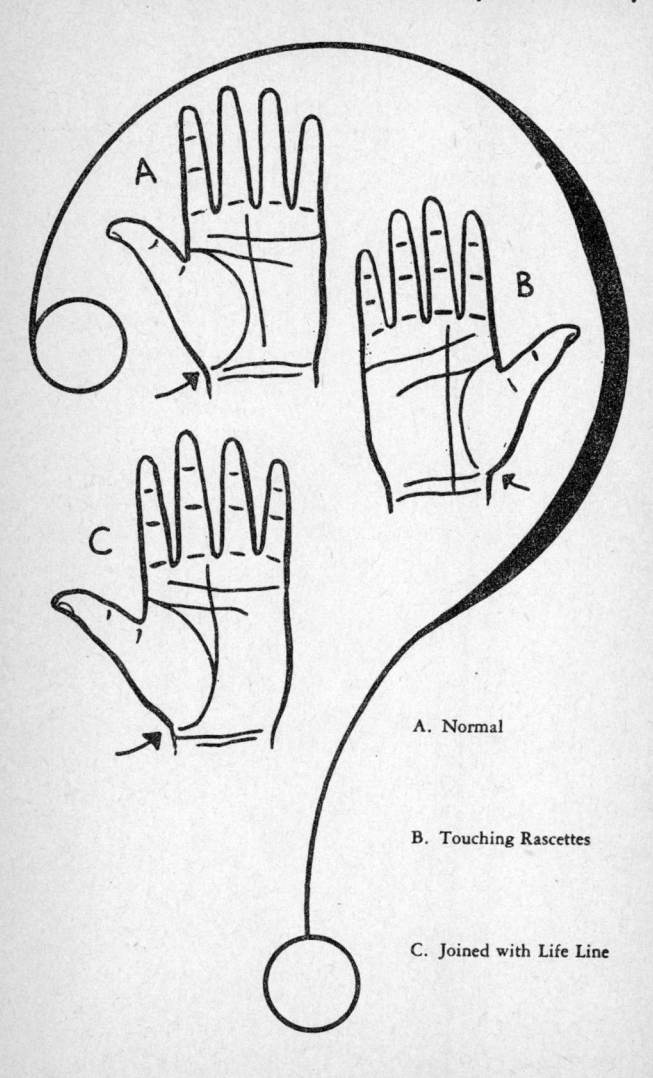

C. Joined with Life Line

Starting Points of the Line of Saturn

The Fate Lines

family. This serves as a booster to success in later years.

Starting from the life Line, there is help from the family, or the career is one that is handed down from one generation to another.

Starting from the Mount of Luna, success and happiness will come from outside sources.

A fork at the start is a handicap of some sort due to parental problems or too vivid an imagination. If the line continues to any one of the Mounts under the fingers, success is inevitable.

TERMINATIONS OF THE LINE OF SATURN

When the Line of Saturn terminates on the Mount of Saturn it is the natural, normal ending for a happy life. If it goes beyond into the second finger, the reverse would take place. This gives unusual power to handle many people or take control of some project but because of an indomitable will and the inability to handle such power, the person eventually falls into disgrace and failure ensues.

Stopping at the Line of Heart, it signifies a disappointment in the affections, causing despondency and ending in failure.

If it terminates on the Head Line, failure is due to faulty judgment.

A forked ending is always a happy one. If one prong goes to Jupiter, a very happy marriage combines with a serious career. If the fork is to Apollo there would be connection

A. On Mount of Saturn

B. On the Line of Heart

C. Forked

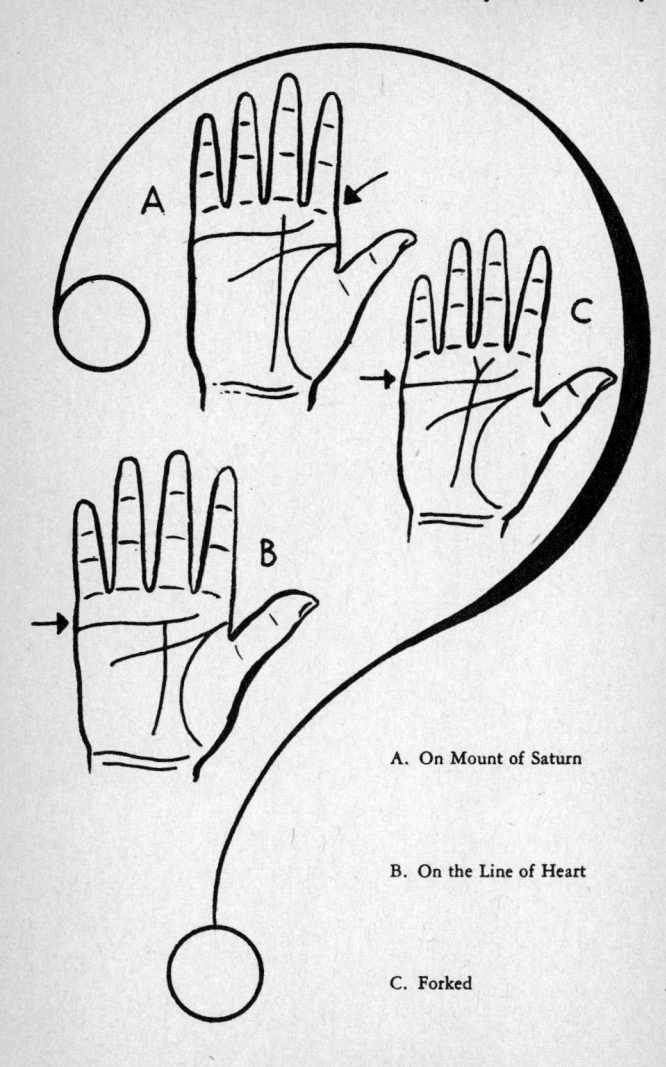

Terminations of the Line of Saturn

The Fate Lines

with some brilliant career in one of the arts. If to Mercury, it would apply to a commercial or professional success.

If the line runs to the Mount of Jupiter instead of Saturn it is complete satisfaction to the ambitions. Nothing more can be asked for or expected.

THE LINE OF APOLLO

The Line of Apollo also starts near the Rascette then proceeds upward to the Mount of Apollo. In its clear normal form it promises fame and money plus a brilliant mind. It is the sign of a natural talent that can be turned into a commercial asset.

Some hands have both Saturn and Apollo. This adds a happy home life as well as the commercial talent.

A single small parallel line on each side of the Line of Apollo directly on the Mount of Apollo strengthens the financial status in old age.

If the line starts from Mount of Luna, the talents would run to poetry, serious music or extraordinary art. From the Mount of Lower Mars, success would be achieved purely from personal efforts.

THE LINE OF MERCURY

This too is another Fate Line. Normally it

128 Key to Palmistry

Endings of the Line of Apollo

With Parallel Lines

Three Prong Fork

Endings of the Line of Mercury

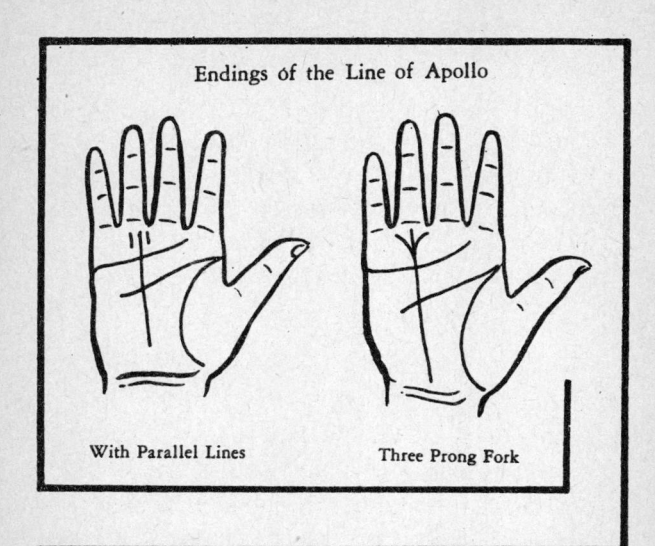

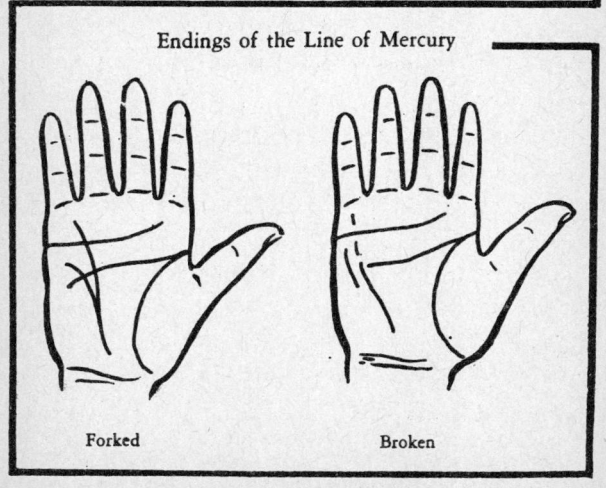

Forked

Broken

Fate Lines

The Fate Lines

starts just above the Rascette and goes directly to the Mount of Mercury. This applies to financial achievement through commerce, science or some profession, such as law, medicine or kindred subjects.

In broken form it indicates health problems. Any overlapping line means recuperation. Branches mean alliances or other interests.

Touching the Line of Apollo

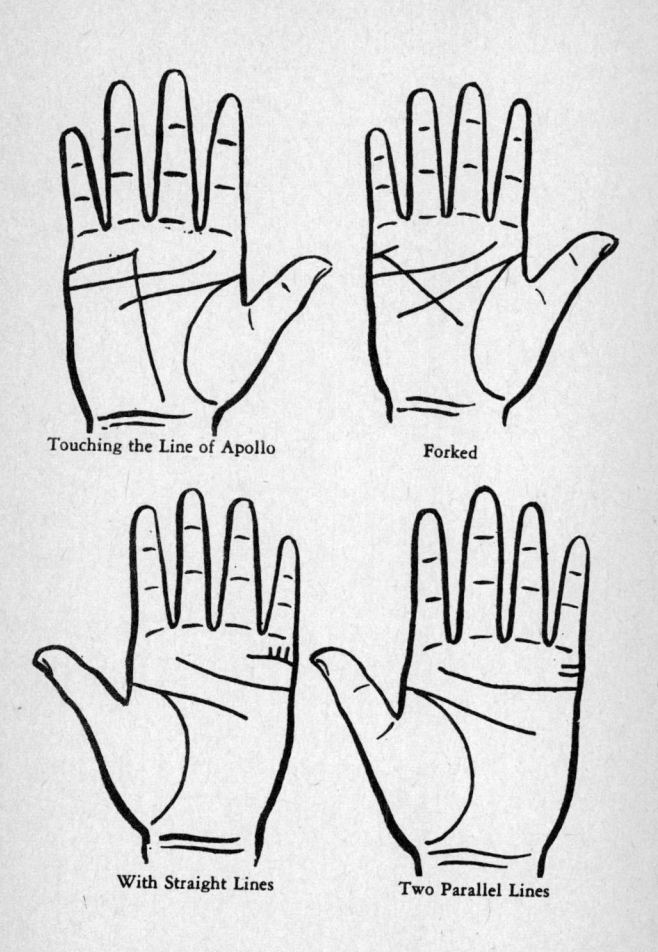

Forked

With Straight Lines

Two Parallel Lines

The Lines of Affection

26
PERCUSSION LINES

These are the horizonal lines that lie beneath the little finger on the Mount of Mercury just above the Heart Line. They start on the percussion of the palm.

If one of these lines goes across the mount and touches the Line of Apollo it means a marriage with a famous person or one who is wealthy.

A forked termination means a separation from a loved one through no fault of self.

An affection line that has straight branches that run toward the little finger promises sons to a family. If the lines slant they are said to mean girls.

A parallel line very close to an affection line is a Sister Line. It means a close affiliation with a member of the family, such as sister, brother, mother, mother-in-law. It also pertains to a friend other than husband or wife.

A long branch that extends across the palm means a separation. If it stops on the fate line it involves money. On the life line, the separation is usually permanent.

A branch to the Mount of Apollo is a brilliant and happy marriage.

Lines of Mars are horizontal percussion lines on Lower Mars that represent struggles. They can be physical such as in combat, boxing, wrestling, or they can pertain to a legal problem.

Travel Lines are the horizontal percussion lines on the Mount of Luna. These are Lesser lines usually short. When they are long enough to extend beyond the area of Luna they become very important. If such a line touches the Life Line, it takes on emotional and physical importance. A person with this combination looks for an escape outlet which can become or already is a vice.

When a travel line touches any of the Fate Lines it has a definite effect on the life of the individual. Plans, surroundings or careers can be affected.

27
THE QUADRANGLE

The Quadrangle is the space that stretches between the Line of Heart and the Line of Head. It should form an evenly shaped quadrangle. The sides are of course imaginary. It must not be narrow at any portion. In its ideal formation it represents an intelligent, well balanced mind. It is indicative of a person who is a loyal friend.

If the space between Heart and Head Line is too wide it indicates a bombastic person who likes to be unconventional, with little regard for religion or morality.

A very narrow Quadrangle means a narrow-minded person, one who has an exalted opinion of his own worth. A very bigoted person with very few friends.

When the widest portion lies under the Mount of Apollo it shows carelessness of personal appearance and business relations.

Many little lines and crosses in this area create a restless nature, one that can become very irritable.

A smooth, unmarked area in the Quadrangle is ideal. It indicates a finely balanced temperament.

Stars are very good, helpful marks within this area when they do not touch a main line. A Star that lies directly beneath Apollo brings fame. Beneath Saturn there is success in a serious profession. If it is below Jupiter it means power. Below Mercury, outstanding achievement in science.

The Quadrangle

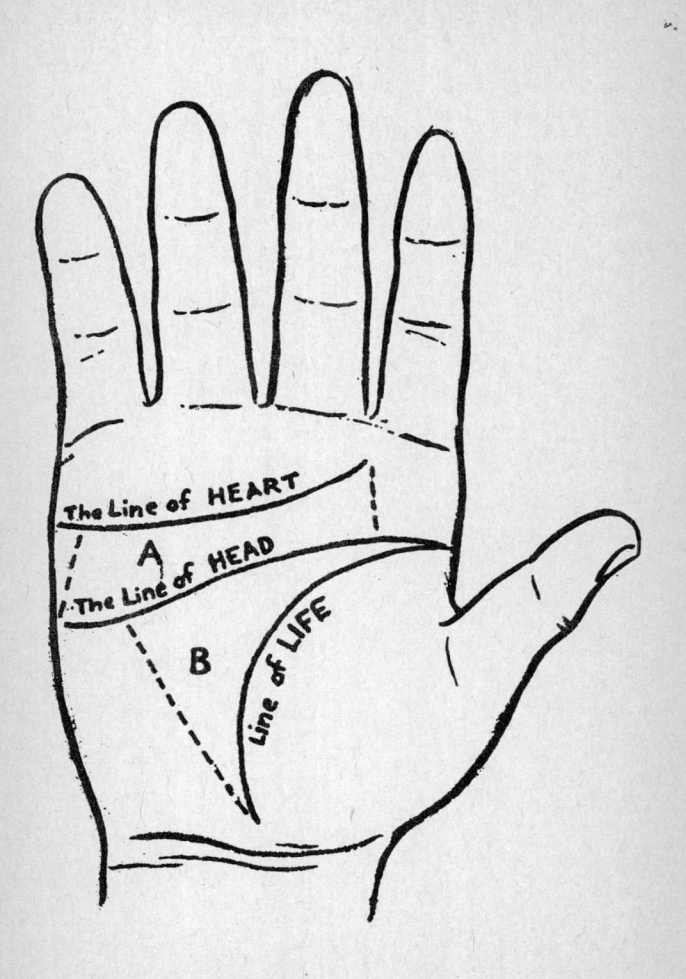

A. The Quadrangle
B. The Great Triangle

28
THE
GREAT
TRIANGLE

The Great Triangle is the space that lies inside the Line of Head, the Line of Life and the Line of Apollo.

When there is no Line of Apollo, use an imaginary line. The Apollo Line or the imaginary one, forms the base of this Great Triangle. If there is a Line of Mercury, it can be used as the base, but it is not as valuable a line. The Apollo Line is the better one for a brilliant powerful success. The Mercury Line produces a more liberal and broadminded person.

Solid lines forming this section mean a beneficient, kindly person. One who will aid a cause, take keen interest in a community project.

Broken or uneven, wavy lines show instability. No strength of purpose. However if the Line of Apollo is a strong line and the Head Line reasonably good, success can be obtained. This indicates that the health would not be strong but it could not interfere with the career.

The Great Triangle takes in the section called the Plain of Mars, which should be checked again to ascertain the depth of the hollow and its relationship to the Mounts.

The Lesser Triangle is formed by the Line of Saturn, the Line of Head and the Line of Mercury, which is also known as the Health Line. If well-defined, this Triangle intensifies a person's talent, signifying that he or she will concentrate that much more on his or her interests.

Sometimes a line which is not well-formed throughout its length, may be strong in relation to either the Great or Lesser Triangle.

When the Line of Mercury is absent, the Line of Apollo (if present) may be considered as a side of the Lesser Triangle.

29
A SAMPLE INTERPRETATION

This is a conic type hand with mixed fingers. The first finger is idealistic. The second adds the seriousness of Saturn. The third is energetic with a flair for anything that is dramatic and colorful. The little finger is long thus giving the ability for business management. The crookedness of the little finger shows that the person is extremely shrewd in money matters and can drive a hard bargain.

The long thin thumb means a very capable mind.

The first phalanges of the fingers and thumb are long, so this places the person in the mental category.

The chained formation at the base of the thumb means an argumentative tendency.

140   Key to Palmistry

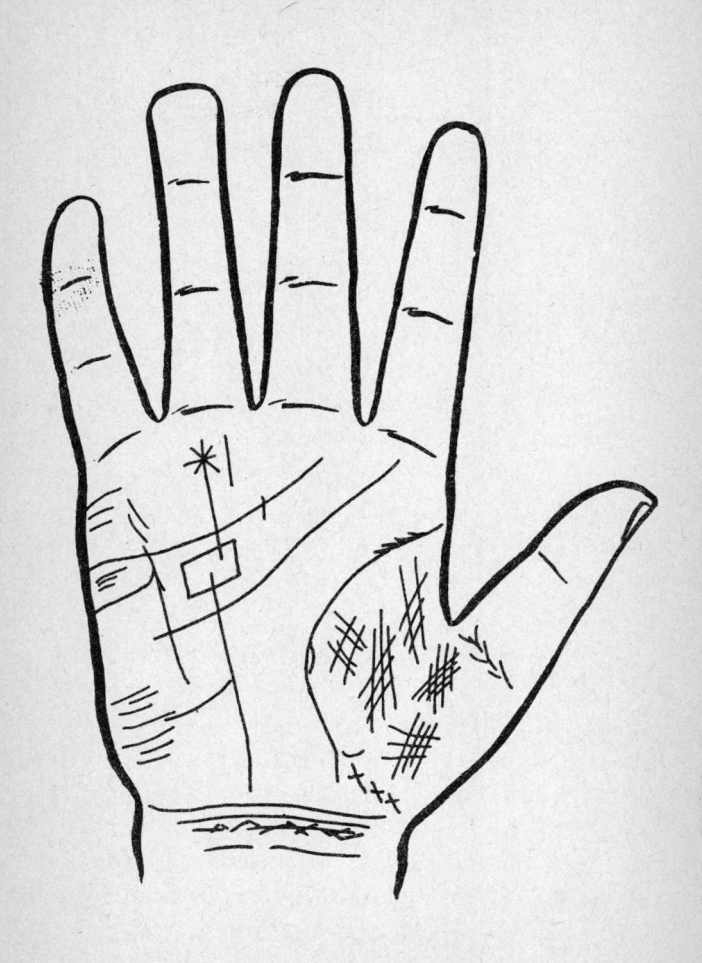

Illustration for Sample Interpretation

A Sample Interpretation

The Mount of Venus is ample and much rayed. This adds an amorous nature. The Mount of Luna has a prominent bulge that means a penchant for travel, adventure and a desire to delve into the realm of imagination. The Mount of Jupiter is exceptionally strong because the Head Line starts on the middle of it. This is ambition for honors and recognition of achievement.

The emotions are controlled by the intellect because the Heart Line is low. The Apollo Line starts on the Rascette showing a struggle during childhood. The same weakness is marked at the start of the Life Line. The Travel Line joins the Apollo Line during youthful years. This gratifies the desire for adventure and travel. The talents are in process here because of the dramatic flair.

The break in the Apollo Line is an accident that interrupts the dramatic career, but the square shows preservation. The Island on the Life Line corroborates this accident. Both lines continue strongly, so the career continues to greater heights. The Star on the end of the Apollo Line is the full realization of a great ambition. The short parallel line confirms the ability for good business acumen and a desire for money.

Like all lives there must be an end. The Mercury Line is broken toward the closing years and the Life Line weakens at the same time.

The end comes gracefully and gloriously.

Now to make a practical reading from this analytical breakdown. First of all this is the hand of a woman who from childhood was serious, intensely active, and the possessor of a very impressionistic mind.

The Line of Apollo plus the spatulate formation of the Apollo finger tell immediately that during childhood she would have dreamed and acted through each day. Her dolls were make believe actors and actresses while she was the star. The early years were filled with illness not unlike many other youngsters, but this only served to give her more time to dream and conjure a whole future though she certainly was not aware of this formative period.

This is the left hand because the person was left handed. Whenever the lines of fulfillment are on the left hand it is to be assumed that the owner is left handed. Also where so much success—as shown on the Line of Apollo—is evident, you know instantly that you are looking at the hands of an important person.

The restlessness shown by the bulge and lines on Luna mean the person has travelled extensively and the line entering the Apollo Line from Luna point to the age, approximately late teen or early 20's when her success was firmly rooted.

Add the argumentative mark of the Thumb Chain and the fine intellect added by the long

A Sample Interpretation 143

slender thumb and you can safely place this hand in the dramatic field which means a theatrical career.

The breaks in the Mercury Line show both ups and downs financially, plus periods of ill health. This is corroborated by the island on the Life Line and the break on the Apollo Line which almost cost her her career. Her indomitable will power and tremendous ambition—shown by the Head Line starting on the Mount of Jupiter—held only boundless limits for her.

Her life was not void of romance. The numerous grilles on the Mount of Venus plus the Affection Lines on the Mount of Mercury give proof on that score.

Her life was long and full. Even her waning health in the last years did not deter her from her greatest love and ambition, that of the theatre. She acted successfully until the end and departed this world as quietly as she entered upon it.